Sour dough from scratch

Sourdough from scratch

James Morton

photography by andy sewell

Hardie Grant

QUADRILLE

Contents

The keys to sourdough

What is sourdough?

Flour, water and salt. Mixed, left and baked.

At its most basic, this is sourdough.

Sourdough, or sourdough bread (*pain au levain*), is what civilised Western man ate before the advent of commercial baker's yeast. Instead, the bread is risen by various wild yeasts and bacteria, cultured spontaneously. The vast majority of these come from the flour itself, where they sit in a dormant state.

The word *sourdough* can refer to the baked loaves of bread, but also to the sourdough starter (levain) – this is a dough of varying wetness that is kept by the baker as a continual fountain of yeast. This makes starting a new **fermentation** a simple and predictable process. Some call this a **mother dough**. And some people name theirs Boris and ask friends to look after it when they go on holiday.

These loaves, compared with ones made using a commercial yeast, usually take longer. Far longer. This has led to a wariness that hangs over even experienced bread makers – sourdough is seen as complicated, involved and with a high risk of failure. For some, this is a turn-off; for others, an allure.

Sourdoughs can usually be identified by the tang that gives them their name, but before then, by their anatomy. Note the smooth and shiny, golden **crust** speckled with tiny bubbles and with a magnificent tear where it has been scored. As you slice through them, you'll witness the **crumb**. This is the word for the pattern of the holes through the middle of your bread. Naturally leavened breads often have large, irregular holes that bounce back when pressed.

The word **sourdough** isn't a protected term. Like craft beer, gin and yoga, it has become an expression of one-upmanship among the hipster elite and something of a middle-class, sabbatical endeavour. It's trendy. It has therefore been jumped on by multinationals, a buzzword for selling upmarket lines at a vastly inflated price. Don't assume 'sourdough' means 'quality'.

The circle of (sourdough) life

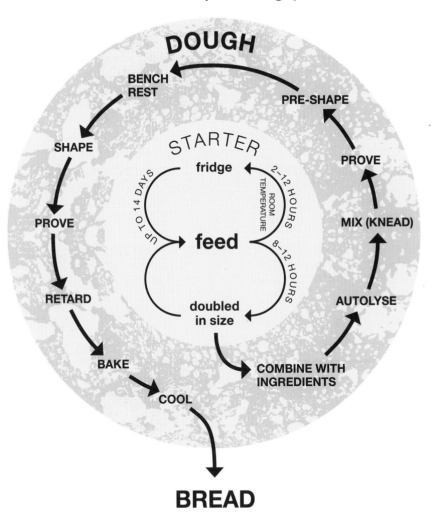

DOUGH

BENCH REST

PRE-SHAPE

SHAPE

PROVE

PROVE

RETARD

MIX (KNEAD)

BAKE

AUTOLYSE

COOL

COMBINE WITH INGREDIENTS

STARTER

fridge

feed

doubled in size

UP TO 14 DAYS

2–12 HOURS ROOM TEMPERATURE

8–12 HOURS

BREAD

The keys to sourdough

A very active starter

Creating a sourdough starter – the thing used to rise your bread – is easy once you know how. We'll cover that. An insufficiently active starter is responsible for the vast majority of sourdough woes, from wet bread pancakes to dense rocks of dough.

If the starter is misbehaving and simply will not rise your bread as it should, don't be sentimental. We'll fix it using science, or dump it because of science. Don't get hung up on keeping it alive if it is suffering. It's very simple to make a new one. And while some bakers will tell you a nice story about the aged nature of their starter, time actually bears no resemblance to quality.

A good starter should always be doubling or tripling in size when fed. If you're not baking bread every day or two (and that's most people), you should keep your starter in the fridge between uses. It can be used as soon as it's warmed up to room temperature again. If you have any doubts about its bubbliness, then you can take it out the night before you use it and give it a good feed.

Good dough strength

Gluten, the wonderful matrix of protein in flour that gives dough its gas-capturing abilities, is developed and sculpted through the stages of bread making. Gluten is often developed by kneading, but this is just one of the many ways, and it certainly isn't the only one we'll use. Sometimes kneading is recommended, but many times it's not. Kneading develops the structure of the gluten, but it doesn't necessarily develop it in the right way.

This property of being able to maintain a shape or structure without degrading is known as **strength**. You should notice your dough is **elastic**, or springy. Leave your dough to rest, and as the gluten slides over itself, it will lose its strength. You'll notice your dough is more **extensible**, or stretchy. If you've made your dough too stiff, with not enough water, or with lots of wholemeal flour, it will be overly **tenacious**, or firm.

By developing good strength through a combination of **mixing**, **stretching**, **folding** and **shaping**, you are avoiding that 'flop' sound you get when bread made from a wet, under-kneaded dough that's poorly shaped hits the work surface.

Warmth

Sourdough goes through the same **proving**, or resting, stages as any bread. After you've weighed and mixed your ingredients, your finished loaf could be four hours away, or a day, or anything in between. This is your choice. The rests allow the yeasts within your sourdough starter to produce carbon dioxide gas, which rises your dough.

On average, sourdough takes two to three times as long to prove as standard yeasted loaves. The first prove takes **three to six hours** at room temperature, depending on what your room temperature is. After you've shaped it, there's at least another **hour or three** of re-filling with bubbles. Despite being a very long process, it should take up only **half an hour of your time**. This means that a busy person can still churn out a lot of bread around a demanding job and family.

It's important to think about **temperature** and how much it is going to influence your dough. While in my first book I maintained that proving dough in a warm place (airing cupboard, or near a heater) was a bad thing, this is not the case for sourdough. My house is quite cold, so I use warm water and put it near a heater to ensure a decent prove. The rapidly expanding, tense bubbles are the architecture that provides your dough with great strength. Without this, your dough will need extra work to keep it together.

Alongside this, you will see the allure of **retarding** your dough in the fridge, overnight or longer. I often do this on the second prove, because this allows me to bake it whenever I feel like it. I'm in control. More importantly, retarding either prove helps develop a lot of flavour and leads to a softer, more irregular crumb.

Be gentle

Between the proves, we use our hands to **shape**. In my last book, I advocated a very traditional, heavy-handed method of shaping, based on old British prejudices. Sourdough shaping and strengthening, however, requires a very light touch. Under no circumstances should one ever 'knock back' the dough, expelling all that precious gas.

If you hit that sweet spot and manage to keep all those big bubbles in there while creating a tight (bouncy) dough, it will appear to have layers of smooth sheets protecting it from sticking to anything. You're going to have bread that rises magnificently in the oven and a beautifully contrasting crust: between the smooth edge and rough '**ears**' where it has expanded.

If your dough doesn't have the strength to hold itself up, you can **pre-shape**, and indeed I recommend this extra step in nearly every recipe. This is an even more delicate shaping process done about half an hour before the main event, and can really help if you've had pancake-shaped loaves in the past.

Steam

The key to amazing **oven spring**, the rise of the bread in the oven, is steam. It's also the key to a golden, shiny crust that's deliciously crisp for the first day, and chewy in the days beyond that. When you bake your bread in the oven, you should find a way to introduce steam.

I used to advocate chucking a glass of water inside the oven, and I'm sorry for the fuses that have been blown as a result. I've since learned that the single best way of introducing steam is by baking your bread under cover – either inside a lidded cast-iron pot, or beneath a cloche or bread bell (a metal or ceramic dome). These trap the steam produced as the loaf bakes until the oven spring is complete, and then you can remove it to develop the crust.

Some shapes of bread don't fit inside a round pot, of course, and so baking on a flat stone or tray is necessary. In this case, I stick a cast-iron griddle pan to preheat on the oven floor and pour water into it as I slide my bread onto the rack above – just remember to remove the pan when you vent the oven if there is any water left in it, so no more steam is created.

Use what you have – I have some old Le Creuset cast-iron pots that my parents got as a wedding present, so that's what I use most often. The lid stays on for the first 20 minutes, and comes off for another 20 minutes to crisp up the crust. For a supremely even crust, I will often bake my bread straight on the oven shelf for a final 10 minutes.

A routine

All of the best sourdough bakers I know rely on a routine: that of doing the same things over and over again. Gradually your technique is refined as you see what works and what doesn't, and we all develop our own path to a better loaf. This doesn't mean baking bread every single day, but it might mean baking bread once a week. Frequency is much less important than consistency. If you change something, make it one thing and measure it.

The need to feed a starter enforces this – if you're having to pour away a starter because you've got too much, think about baking a little more. The only issue with this is that it can become rather addictive. Neighbours, colleagues and family will always be very appreciative, though.

A note on measurements

My dear American cousins: one day you'll come to love the metric system, at least in part, as we now do in Britain. To facilitate this transition, I recommend you tackle every recipe with a set of good digital scales and in grams. Your accuracy and thus your baking ability will improve. You'll find some helpful translations of common terms in this book, but other quirky 'Britishisms' can be deciphered through a quick Google search.

Equipment & ingredients

Equipment

You don't need much kit to make bread. The items required for good, consistent sourdough make for a short list: an oven is a solid start, followed by a bowl, a set of electronic scales, something sharp with which to score the bread and a tea towel (dish towel). The only other thing you'll need is a surface to bake on, which could be anything from an oven tray to a heatproof pot. Most people have all of this in their kitchens already.

This wee section will go through each piece of equipment that you might want and some minimum requirements to look out for, along with a few entertaining musings, if you're lucky.

Oven

Ovens can be separated into a few categories: gas or electric, fan or conventional. Whichever you have doesn't matter, as great bread can be made in any oven.

The ways to modify an oven for better bread are numerous – the best is to bake your bread inside a **cloche** or **pot** (see page 20). The next best is to use a **baking stone**. A granite slab will even out your heat distribution and help your loaves expand from the bottom up, but radically increase your preheating time: at least 40 minutes before baking. Then, when you slide your bread onto it, your oven will have relatively little work to do. Combined with the use of water to create some steam, you'll get fantastic oven spring.

If you're lucky enough to have an **Aga** or **Rayburn**, you can bake great bread by sliding it onto the floor of the hot oven. If you find that your bases burn too easily, then place a baking stone directly onto the floor of the oven.

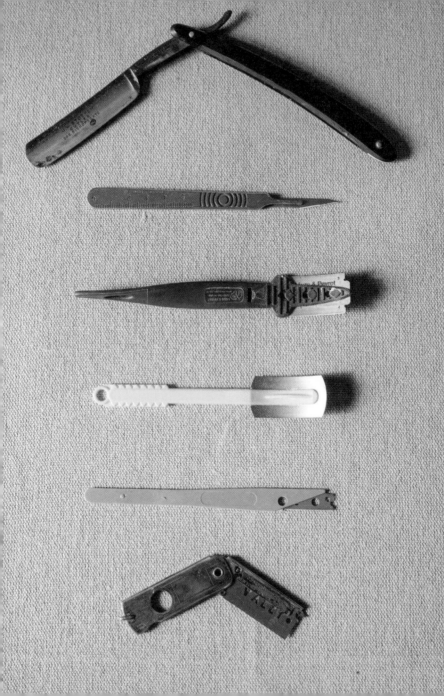

Dough scraper

Almost as essential as the oven, the dough scraper is a wonderful thing. You might have one already, or a selection. Some of you might have soft silicone things that resemble dough scrapers – these are rubbish. You want to stick to hard plastic, and if you can, have one that's stainless steel, too. The latter is known as a 'dough knife' or 'Scotch scraper' and is good for dividing large batches of dough into individual portions and for scraping surfaces down after kneading or shaping.

The former – the plastic, mildly malleable but mostly rigid device – can be used for the above, but doesn't do quite as good a job. But if you're going to have one dough scraper, then make it a plastic one, simply for the sake of something that's multipurpose. It's excellent for scooping dough from one place to another, for kneading, and for scraping clean bowls, or scales, or your hands, for that matter – it's your tool to help you rule the bread making world.

Scales

Get yourself some basic electronic scales. This isn't so that you can get your hydration (wetness) bang on – this doesn't matter much – it's so that you can get accurate salt levels; often in bread we sail quite close to the threshold of 'too salty' because we want the maximum flavour and strength possible. That means that even half a gram or one gram more in a loaf can taint it.

Standard electronic scales from the supermarket or your local homeware shop aren't that accurate, but they are good enough. They also tend to come with a fantastic warranty, so stick the receipt in the box and keep it – I find they often break within a year or two.

For salt I use scales I bought from a dubious supply store on eBay that measure to 0.01g. I hold my hands up and admit that this is another hipster indulgence. You don't need to be that exact.

Proving basket

A basket is there to support your dough, to add a pretty pattern and to allow you to cover the dough and stop it drying out.

It isn't an essential, but it's very much recommended. The main reason is that a basket helps to regulate the structure of the dough – as your loaf rises, more gas forms in bubbles towards the top of the dough. When you bake the dough, the bubbles on top tend to expand more than the ones on the bottom. The proving basket means that your dough is flipped upside down just before baking, regulating the above phenomena.

Baskets aren't expensive, but you can make one out of a tea towel and a bowl if you're feeling tight. If you choose to invest in one, you'll hear a few names bandied about, such as **brotform** and **banneton**. These terms are all interchangeable: my favourite baskets are 'wood fibre brotforms', because I find them least likely to stick.

Couche

A couche is a heavy piece of linen. It is used in a similar way to a proving basket in that it supports the sides of dough. It must be dusted heavily in flour. A couche is used primarily with baguettes and batons – these long cylinders of dough are lined up in parallel with a fold of floured material in between each, so they support each other as they prove. They work well for very wet doughs like ciabatta, too, but you've got to make sure they're properly coated in flour.

Thick, coarse linen is good because it has a tendency not to stick and its stiffness provides some support in itself, but you can create your own just by using any large piece of material – a heavy tea towel will also work.

Trays, tins, pots and stones

You'll need something to bake your bread on, or in.

The traditional baking surface is the stone, and it is one that I've used on and off for many years. The idea is to try to emulate the conditions of a traditional baker's oven; the stone absorbs a lot of heat, meaning that even through the opening and shutting of the oven door and the placing of a cold slab of dough on top, it stays hot. This surface transfers heat directly into the dough, giving an awesome base and good oven spring.

You can use a baking stone to even out the temperature in a temperamental oven, but it does takes ages to heat up. If you don't preheat for 40 minutes or more before using it, the sub-temperature stone will actually cool the dough compared to the rest of the oven, giving you a soggy, dense base.

If you have a cast-iron pot or Dutch oven, you can exactly recreate the environment found in a professional baker's oven; Le Creuset or any knock-offs will do. Be wary, though, that temperatures over 220°C (430°F) will cause the outer enamel of your pots to darken.

Preheated, your loaf will take 20 minutes with the lid on and then 30 minutes with the lid off. I find you get a more even crust by splitting it 20-20-10: 20 minutes lid on, 20 minutes lid off, and then finish it directly on the oven shelf for 10 minutes. Choosing not to preheat the pot is legitimate, and this is a technique you can use to further save energy and help bake multiple loaves in succession. I do find that oven spring and dough flavour is slightly better using a hot pot, though.

You'll see ceramic cloches advertised, and these do a good job. But not, in my experience, quite as good a job as the cast-iron ones or cast-iron pots, in terms of crust colour and oven spring. These are also fragile: you should preheat them in the oven, as placing a cold ceramic cloche in a hot oven can cause it to crack.

Equipment

Proving baskets

Peel

Steel dough scraper

Scales, plastic dough scraper

Something sharp

Scoring bread is an art, and we will get onto that, but first, you'll need something with which to score it (see page 17). To begin with, your sharpest knife will have to do. If you're an obsessive Japanese knife enthusiast with razor-sharp blades, you need look no further, as these will be more than adequate. If not, serrated 'tomato knives' are a pretty good place to start, as they slice through the skin of a dough with minimal tug.

If you or a loved one shaves using a traditional safety razor with a double-sided blade, this is the perfect blade for scoring bread. You have to be careful, though. They do make excellent tools, but they are dangerous. I once left one lying around, wrapped loosely in its paper wrapping. My mother grabbed it thinking it was a scrap of paper, slicing into her palm and several fingers.

These razor blades can be transformed into safe(r) scoring devices known as a *lame* (it's French, pronounced like 'lamb'). This is a handle that holds your blade securely. It's worth picking one up, if not for the safety guard alone, but you can also make your own by curving your razor blade around a chopstick or skewer.

Peel

A peel is used to transfer dough from one place to another, and sometimes used to retrieve loaves from deep inside ovens.

If you bake using a stone, you will need something to transfer your dough onto for scoring, and then to use for sliding the dough into the oven and onto the hot stone. While there are a great many purpose-designed peels available for home use, they aren't necessary. A thin baking sheet, while not good for baking bread on, makes a great peel. This allows you to slide right underneath your dough without causing any trauma.

Whatever form your peel takes, it should be dusted with a little semolina, rather than flour. The roughly ground durum wheat acts like little ball bearings for sliding and gives you a very crispy crust.

Mixer

You definitely don't need an electric mixer, but it can be quite a nice thing to have, especially if you have a health condition that makes kneading difficult, or you're lazy. Lots of us have one sitting pretty without much use, so it's nice to be able to put it through its paces.

Ingredients

Flour

What is flour? Flour is anything that's edible and floury. Most often, I'm talking about ground up cereals. After grinding, or milling, you are left with **wholemeal flour**. This means that the whole 'meal' remains: nothing is taken away. Simple. And if wheat happens to be the cereal used, that's called **wholewheat flour.**

Following this, most flour goes through a refining process of some kind; this makes it whiter. Refining the flour involves removing some of the bran and the germ. The simplest way of doing this is by using a sieve. Larger grades of sieve will remove just the big bits of bran and leave you with a flour that is somewhere between brown and white. Using a very fine sieve will not allow any of the brown stuff through, and you get something akin to **white flour**. Bran absorbs a lot of additional moisture. Therefore, if you do use wholemeal flours in your breads, you should be adding significantly more water when formulating your recipes. I also like to do a long rest before kneading (called an **autolyse** – see page 46) when using more wholemeal flour, to give the bran time to soak up as much water as possible.

Gluten

Good bread is normally made with **strong flour**. This means it has more of certain proteins – two of these proteins, called glutenin and gliadin, form a complex, sponge-like matrix when tangled together. This matrix is **gluten**, the wonderful pantomime villain of the 'wellness' industry. If you understand gluten, you will understand bread.

Gluten is awesome. It is the building block of bread. Making truly good gluten-free bread is difficult because the gluten provides a structure that can be manipulated into something that can then be shaped and moved without losing aeration – it has resilience. Indeed, as the initially random gluten structure is stretched and folded through the process of kneading, it becomes more organised, moving from a random sticky mess into thousands of overlapping, flexible sheets of protein.

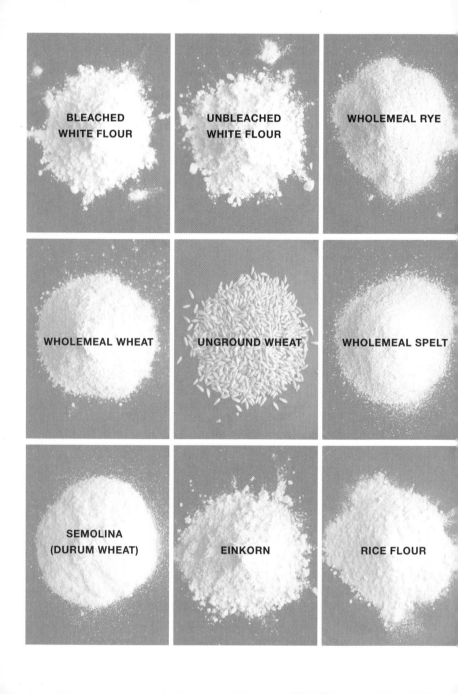

As your yeasts munch away on the starch in the flour, they produce carbon dioxide gas. This gas would simply escape from the dough if it wasn't for the gluten – but instead it is captured by these organised sheets of protein and contained. The pressure from the gas further develops the structure of the dough and can aid in reinforcing its structure. Too much pressure, though, and the bonds that help form the gluten matrix collapse, leading to burst bubbles and a flat loaf. This is what happens if you leave your dough for too long, or too hot.

Common cereals

Wheat, or common wheat, is the third most widely cultivated grain in the world, after maize and rice. Wheat is wonderful. It doesn't just provide an enormous proportion of the world's nutrition, it forms the basis for nearly all of my recipes because it has been the backbone of the bread that has built the Western world. There's a huge variety, and white flours range between 8% protein (sponge flour) to 16% protein (very strong Canadian-grown flour). Some are even fortified with further gluten to facilitate greater structure and easier handling.

Durum wheat is the species of wheat used to make **semolina**. Durum has a very hard endosperm, meaning that it is difficult and time consuming to mill it into flour. Semolina is therefore usually sold as coarse granules and is very useful for adding texture and acting as tiny, crispy ball bearings that stop your bread doughs sticking to surfaces.

Spelt is a subtype of wheat. Its popularity has been driven by its nutty flavour, but also by the people who cling to the idea that it has been consistently cultivated for at least 7,000 years, without significant genetic engineering during this time. Proponents of spelt argue that the natural goodness of wheat is somehow lost by breeding it, which is unproven in any kind of rigorous way. Either way, spelt is tasty, and so I use it. Spelt is high-protein, often more than 20%, but contains less gluten than wheat.

Rye is awesome. It has a deeply earthy, spicy and slightly astringent flavour that works well with the light flavour of wheat. It's difficult to make a 100% rye bread with good aeration, as it has a thick bran and a very low gluten content. When I wrote my first book, you could only find rye in some of the bigger and posher supermarkets – now I'm delighted to say it's a staple.

Barley is used to make beer, but you can use it equally well to make bread. In small quantities, it adds a nuttiness. **Einkorn** and **Khorasan** (Kamut) are a couple of the more commercially well known of the many varieties of ancient wheat available. **Buckwheat**, confusingly, isn't wheat – it's a dried seed from a rhubarb-like plant. It's good for making noodles, pasta and, of course, crêpes, but also for adding a little into your bread.

Water

There's everything and nothing to say about water. Without water, your dough can't ferment, and your gluten can't form. Water is good. Sometimes it's a helpful endeavour, for the sake of simplicity, to set certain rules around water; for example, to always strive to use more of it ('wetter is better'). Or use water that is only cool to tepid, and never hot. Follow these rules if bread making is new to you or these are unfamiliar concepts, and your bread may improve. The truth is that these are only true up to a point and there are no rules except one: **use your tap**.

No matter how filthy your tap water is, no matter how hard, no matter how much it has been recycled through the digestive tracts of other human beings and no matter how many self-righteous blogs tell you to use bottled water – use your tap. Tap water is fine for making bread. How 'hard' your tap water is will affect the structure and the fermentation a bit, but not much. The traditional teaching is that hard water helps with yeast growth and fermentation and adds to dough strength – and this is correct. But it isn't something that can't be dealt with in soft-water areas by waiting a little longer or giving your dough an extra fold. I can assure you there is not enough of a difference to require your giving much thought to it, presuming you are working at a sub-industrial scale, as most of us are.

If contamination of your water is an issue, this will not matter because the bread is going to be baked and any worrying bacteria will be dead. If the opposite is true and your water is very chlorine-heavy and sterile, equally, don't worry. Even when present in massive quantities, the only effect it might have is to slow down your fermentation, but I find that the bugs that thrive in my sourdough starter don't seem to mind too much.

Salt

In bread, salt is first a flavour enhancer, as it is in all food, but its second effect is on the preservation of your dough. Salt preserves because it attracts water – this means that any troublesome bacteria or moulds nearby have less water in which to grow. This water-holding capacity also maintains moisture in the bread; a salt-free bread stales within a day.

Salt adds strength – in part because it competes with the flour in attracting water, but also because it strengthens the bonds between the proteins that make up the gluten. While this strength makes the dough a bit easier to handle, it can also lengthen mixing and proving times. The increased resistance of a stronger gluten matrix from the start lengthens the process of flattening out that gluten into nice sheets ready to be filled. This makes mixing harder and longer, and as a result many bakers choose to leave out the salt for the first part of the resting and even some of the kneading process.

For dough, use cheap salt. What we want in bread is something that is dissolved easily and quickly, and the cheap, small-granule industrial stuff is perfect for this. We want the sodium chloride and we don't want any of the impurities that allegedly give extra flavour in posh salt.

Sugars

I don't add sugar to any of my savoury bread doughs, and find the idea of adding it routinely to sourdough a little strange. Adding table sugar, or sucrose, is a cheat used by legendarily bad British bakers in order to obtain a golden crust in as little time as possible. In sourdough, the long fermentation and mix of organisms mean that lots of starch is broken down into sugar naturally. There's plenty to help caramelise our crusts and leave that sweet tang that helps sourdough taste so good.

Fats

Adding oil, butter or other fat-containing ingredients will have a profound effect on the structure of your dough. Add too much or too early and they will make creating your gluten matrix an absolute pain – how oil lubricates a car engine is exactly how it lubricates between the protein molecules. Rather than getting an ever-expanding gluten matrix, you get an ever-sliding mass of globules.

You can overcome this with lots of mixing, but it will take a fair while. Therefore, if you are adding lots of oil or butter to your dough, add it after the mixing is complete, or at least towards the end of it. As a general rule, if the weight of fat is less than 5% of the weight of flour, it can be added safely at the beginning. If it's above this, it's best to leave it until the end.

Chunk and bits

The great thing about bread is the freedom for experimentation. Once you're happy with the basics, you can go one of two ways – the first is to get really, really into the science of it and absolutely perfect your crust, your scoring or crumb structure. The second is to go wild by customising your bread with various flavours – nuts, seeds, dried fruit, spices, herbs and so on.

The issue with extras is that they physically get in the way of the structure of the gluten. For larger ingredients such as dried fruit and nuts, this isn't so much a problem because the matrix holds them in suspense and expands around them. Incorporating these is pretty easy – add them all at once at the end of the kneading or mixing stage, or during your lamination (see page 56). If you add them right at the start, they do get in the way, impacting on the formation of those nice regular sheets of gluten.

Smaller ingredients, such as the more hardy herbs, whole spices and small seeds (like poppy seeds or sesame seeds) cause a bigger issue. Adding them too early in your bread-making process prolongs the gluten development. Adding them too late means they won't be mixed in properly, or you'll remove any dissolved CO_2 in your dough in the mixing process. And these extras do rather get in the way, leading, inevitably, to slightly smaller, thicker bubbles compared to a dough without them.

A country loaf from scratch

The principles

How to start a rye sourdough starter: the short version

Flour and liquid
Mix about 100g rye flour and 100g fruit juice (pineapple, grapefruit, apple or orange) in a container and wait. If you don't have juice, just use water.

Mix and wait
Mix twice daily for 5 days until it starts to become very aerated. Don't add more flour. Ignore any bubbles in the first couple of days.

Feed
When the aerated starter begins to contract, add at least another 100g each of rye flour and water. Leave it for a final half-day until it rises again. Now, move it to the fridge and feed weekly.

You can't make sourdough without a sourdough starter. This is the microbiological gift that rises and flavours your bread. The simplest way of starting one is getting one from someone else. But then it won't be yours. It won't be unique. Start one yourself, at least once.

This process takes about a week.

When you create your starter, you're reawakening the multitude of bacteria and yeast lying dormant within the grain. They start to break down the starch into sugars, which they then use to grow and multiply. The yeast works intimately with the bacteria to produce **carbon dioxide** (CO_2), which rises the bread, and some alcohol and some acid, which sours the bread. With these, there are loads of flavourful compounds – some desirable, and some less so.

How to start a rye sourdough starter: the long version

1. Flour and liquid

Mix about 100g rye flour and 100g fruit juice (pineapple, grapefruit, apple or orange) in a container and wait. If you don't have juice, just use water.

Your choice of flour is crucial. These rules apply to any cereal and you can use wheat or spelt if you want to, but I've had most consistent results with rye flour. **Organic, stoneground, wholemeal rye flour.** The majority of posh rye flours you'll find in the supermarket will fit the bill. Ideally, support someone local and independent who gets the flour straight from the miller, and who can assure you it is fresh.

Find a receptacle in which to store your starter. A piece of Tupperware, a Kilner (Mason) jar, a sturdy drinking glass covered loosely with cling film (plastic wrap): anything. My humble favourite is the jam (jelly) jar – just make sure you leave the lid loose, or it might explode. It helps if your receptacle is glass or transparent plastic so that you can see what's going on.

There's no great need to weigh – the quantities of flour and liquid should be roughly equal. I'm deliberately vague here – it matters little the scale, and it matters less the exact ratio. For those who feel more comfortable with an exact quantity, follow the measures above.

I'm suggesting fruit juice because I've had more consistent results by doing it this way. The science is interesting – the acid in the juice suppresses some unwanted fermentations and so you've got a higher chance of culturing the right bugs first time. It's nothing to do with the sugar in the juice.

cont.

In my own (albeit crude) experimentation, juice has been especially helpful when using cheap supermarket flour.

Once you've mixed your flour and liquid, stick a loose-fitting lid (or lay cling film) over your starter receptacle and leave it somewhere at about room temperature: 18–22°C (65–72°F) is perfect. If it's hotter, then things will happen faster, but don't stick it on a radiator or in the sunlight. If it's colder than 18°C (65°F) at home, you might need to add a day or two onto this entire process.

If using fruit juice, it's vitally important to stir at least once daily, if not twice, to stop mould growth.

2. Mix and wait

Mix your starter twice daily for 5 days until it starts to become very aerated. Don't add more flour. Ignore any bubbles in the first couple of days.

After a day or so, give it a stir. You might notice a few bubbles. Ignore these; they're probably caused by a little air being introduced during stirring. Don't add any more flour.

On day three, you might notice an exciting number of bubbles at this point, or this might take another day. Ignore these, too. **These bubbles are caused by an early bacterial fermentation that is no good for making bread with.** These are not the bugs you want to grow. Do not add more flour. Stir away the bubbles and then leave it.

Days three and four are generally the same. A few more bubbles, maybe, but the bubbles might stop altogether when the bacteria that caused them starts to falter as the starter becomes more and more sour. The mixture will appear wetter. Do not add any more flour or water. Continue to stir gently daily, or twice a day if you can be bothered.

On roughly the fifth or sixth day (but it might be anything from the fourth to the seventh) you'll notice a distinct rise in the number of bubbles and a big jump in the volume of your starter. Now we're getting somewhere, and you can move to the next stage.

If you don't notice this increase after a full week has passed, or if your starter turns **black** or **pink** or **blue** or you notice a very strong, unpleasant smell, dump it and begin again. This doesn't usually happen if you use good flour. If you're really struggling, consult the starter troubleshooting guide later on.

3. Feed

When the aerated starter begins to contract, add at least another 100g each of rye flour and water. Leave it for a final half-day until it rises again. Now, move to the fridge and feed weekly.

Feeding is the process of keeping your starter alive in perpetuity by adding more flour and water. Don't use juice again – tap water is fine. Your starter can be kept at room temperature, and in this case it will need to be fed every day or, at a minimum, every two days. If you keep your starter in the fridge, it should be fed weekly to keep it active, but it will easily survive several weeks between feeds.

Once your starter has made its big jump in volume, try not to feed it straight away. Let it get used to this new environment. Let the bugs grow. Feeding it with new flour at this stage will radically alter this new ecosystem. When you notice the walls of the bubbles begin to collapse or the volume start to diminish, that's when you can be confident that you've got as much yeast as you're going to and you can feed it.

Feed it with equal quantities of rye flour and water. Stir well. A few hours after, you'll notice some new bubbles. It will begin to rise again. Over the next 12 hours it will rise to at least double the size of where you started after adding the extra flour and water. Make sure there's plenty of space for this, or transfer to a more suitable jar or receptacle.

Your sourdough starter is now ready. As a rule, it should be fed in proportions similar to those aforementioned – the **new total weight** of starter should be at least **double** that prior to feeding. You can go as high as triple or quadruple comfortably. Much higher (for example, if you use all the starter and restart it just from what's stuck to the sides) and you'll notice that your starter takes a long time to kick off its fermentation – it might take a couple of days at room temperature to get going properly again after this.

If you feed it only in small volumes, your starter will use the new flour in a short time, and will gradually become more and more acidic. To maintain good activity, you'd need to feed more regularly.

A final note about storing in the fridge: when we use our cold starter, we let it warm up to room temperature first. This allows the yeast to acclimatise. When feeding, it also helps to do this at room temperature. It's then good practice to leave your starter out of the fridge for a few hours so that the fermentation can get underway. When you notice the first bubbles, you can safely stow it cold.

Sourdough formula: steps

If your sourdough starter seems in good health following the first feed, then you can use it to make great bread without any manipulation or delay. If it has been sitting about in the fridge for **anything over a week** without being fed, it's best to take it out, let it rise to room temperature and give it a good feed the night before you're planning on baking.

Some bakers formalise this process by feeding the required amount of starter in a separate container to create a ***levain*** (which is just French for sourdough). This misnomer of a pre-dough is made 6–14 hours before you mix your initial dough. Either making a separate levain or giving your starter a good feed the night before ensures that your starter bugs are extremely healthy prior to use.

Ingredients for 1 large loaf

450g strong white flour, plus extra for dusting
300g tepid-warm water
100g rye sourdough starter
10g table salt
semolina, for dusting

For multiple loaves, scale this recipe as required.

cont.

Steps

Weigh

In a bowl sitting on top of your scales, weigh your flour, water and starter. Mix together and leave to rest for 30 minutes.

Mix

Add your salt. Knead your dough for 5–10 minutes, or until supple, stretchy and elastic. If you don't want to or can't knead, instead you can do extra stretches and folds (see below) through the first prove.

First prove (bulk prove)

Allow your dough to rest in a covered bowl in a warm place for about 4 hours, or until increased by at least 50% in size. This can be extended, after a couple of hours, by placing the dough in the fridge for up to 1 day.

Stretch, fold and lamination

Increase strength by stretching and folding your dough within its bowl once or twice during the first prove. Alternatively, avoid kneading altogether by carrying this out four or more times during the first *prove*.

Pre-shape and shape

Turn your dough out onto an unfloured surface. Pre-shape into a rough ball and leave to rest for 20–30 minutes. Form into your final shape and place your loaf in a floured proving basket.

Second prove

Rest your dough for a further hour. Alternatively, you can prove in the fridge.

Score

Turn your dough out onto a semolina-dusted peel (tray) and score using a very sharp knife, razor blade or lame.

Bake

Bake your loaf in a very hot preheated oven by sliding into a pot, cloche or Dutch oven, or onto a baking stone. Add steam or bake with the lid or cloche on for 20 minutes before removing the lid and baking for another 20–30 minutes.

Cool

Place your loaf on a cooling rack or wooden board. Allow to cool to just-warm before slicing.

Sourdough formula: explained

1. Weigh

In a bowl sitting on top of your scales, weigh your flour, starter and water. Mix together and leave to rest for 30 minutes.

The first step is to weigh your ingredients. I pop a bowl onto my electronic scales, weigh my flour, zero it, weigh my water, zero it, and finally I weigh out my starter. I usually feed the remainder of my starter at this point, too, so I don't forget to replenish what I've taken from it.

I'll use any number of implements – often my right hand, often a wooden spoon, often a dough hook that's going to get dirty soon anyway – to roughly mix the ingredients together. This is less kneading, more amalgamating into something resembling a very sticky dough.

Next, a rest. Just a short one. Known as an **autolyse**, this rest really increases the stretchability (or extensibility) of your dough, and shortens the time it takes for it to come together. The effect of this rest appears to be rather heightened if you leave the salt out, so that's what we do. Give it 30 minutes, or up to an hour if you can, covered with a damp tea towel.

The quantities here make a loaf of '70% hydration'. This means the total weight of water (350g, because your starter is half water) divided by the total weight of flour (500g) is 0.7, or 70%. This makes a manageable dough, but as you get more used to wet doughs, you'll want to push this higher, for a lighter and softer final bread. I might make the above recipe using up to 425g water, or 85% hydration, depending on the strength of my flour. The first time you try this, you'll think I'm mad. But not one day.

2. Mix

Add your salt. Knead your dough for 5–10 minutes, or until supple, stretchy and elastic. If you don't want to or can't knead, instead you can do extra stretches and folds (see page 54) through the first prove.

First things first: don't forget to add the salt. This is probably the most common mistake at this point, and it is often not realised until the loaf is baked. To avoid this, I leave my salt next to my mixing bowl to remind me.

Great sourdough can be made without any kneading; however, I will say that it's fun and enlightening and good for the bread if you do get your hands dirty and give your dough a slap around. At this stage, you can use your electric mixer – if you do, give your ingredients about 6 minutes on the slowest speed, and then 4 minutes at speed setting '2'. For the most common mixer brands, these numbers equate.

If you are kneading by hand, you can do it a couple of ways. The first is my old chum, the **slap and fold** (see page 50). This is now often referred to as the **Bertinet method** after legendary baker and top bloke Richard Bertinet; it's an old French method of kneading that allows you to handle really sticky doughs, as most in this book are. The second method is a variation on a traditional **English knead** (see page 49). This works a little less well with wet doughs, but if you keep the dough moving, it won't stick too much. Both methods require a dough scraper.

There's one important rule of kneading, or stretching and folding: **Never, ever add flour**, unless you realise you've made a mistake with your quantities. Adding flour makes the dough drier and the final bread tougher. When flour is added later in the knead, it isn't fully hydrated, and so this interrupts your gluten network and reduces the stretchiness of your dough. This is bad. If your dough is sticking to everything, that's okay. Just use your scraper to scrape it all back together into a lump.

You know you're done kneading when your dough has changed from being a sticky, lumpy mess to something that is very smooth, supple and a little bit rubbery.

Following kneading, scrape your dough and any straggly bits back into your bowl. The dirty bowl from mixing is fine. Cover with a damp cloth, or a piece of cling film (plastic wrap), or a plastic supermarket bag. This is just to stop the surface drying out too much.

To clear your hands of dough, grab a bit of flour, rub it between your fingers and then rub all over your hands. The dough will flake off, then your hands can be washed clean more easily.

Kneading: the English knead

1. Turn your dough onto an unfloured surface

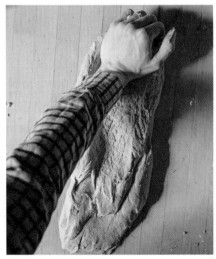

2. Stretch the dough away from you

3. Use the same hand to scoop and roll the dough towards you

4. Repeat, occasionally turning the dough 90 degrees

Kneading: the slap and fold

1. Scrape your dough out of your bowl onto an unfloured surface

2. Slide your fingers underneath the dough

3. Lift the dough in the air

4. Turn it over and slap it down

Kneading: the slap and fold (continued)

5. Grab the end that's facing towards you

6. Stretch it towards you and fold it over

7. Turn the dough around a quarter turn and repeat

8. Use your scraper to incorporate any excess

3. First prove (bulk prove)

Allow your dough to rest in a covered bowl in a warm place for about 4 hours, or until increased by at least 50% in size. This can be extended, after a couple of hours, by placing the dough in the fridge for up to 1 day.

It is likely that the recipe on the back of your flour packet does not recommend proving your dough twice. But I do, and so does every other sourdough baker. The first rest, or prove, following kneading and before shaping, is absolutely necessary for reasons including, but not limited to, the following:

- It gives a great, golden crust. The extra time proving prior to shaping allows the bacteria and yeast to break down more starch into sugar, giving a sweeter, softer inside, or **crumb.** And this means that there are more sugars at the edge, too, so more to caramelise on the crust when the bread is baked.

- It makes the bread taste awesome. The yeast and bacteria, and a huge number of other bacteria and yeast that live in symbiosis with their domineering cousins, all produce certain flavours – so give them a chance to.

- It develops the gluten. This is the primary reason for giving your bread a chance to prove twice. Kneading will develop the gluten into nice linear sheets, but those sheets need to fill with the carbon dioxide produced from your yeast. These bubbles tighten the gluten and give it structure, as well as passing it over its neighbouring strands and further improving the immense matrix.

- It gives you an open structure. A good, long first prove is crucial for achieving a really nice, aerated crumb: the signature of sourdough.

This is why when we shape our bread, we do it very gently indeed, so as not to destroy the bubbles we've created following the first prove. The preservation of these, with the added strength of shaping, allows them to grow rather large.

How long the first prove will be is usually determined by the temperature. A good rule is to prove it at a warmer-than-room temperature of 25°C (77°F) or so, for 3–4 hours. The traditional teaching is that it should double in volume, but this is a very difficult measurement to make, especially if you're stretching and folding (see page 54). And if you're waiting for a dense wholemeal or rye dough to double, you'll be waiting all day. An increase in size of roughly 50% is more than adequate for most loaves.

The great thing about bread, though, is the malleability of the process, meaning you can make it as and when to suit your lifestyle. Say, for example, you want to extend that 3–4 hour prove, as you're out at some sort of social engagement for 6–7 hours; no problem, as you can mix your dough with cold water instead of warm to delay (retard) your fermentation.

Bakeries use large retarders to delay their fermentations; these are expensive, many-shelved fridges. You can use your own fridge, and doing so will have a tremendous effect on the flavour of your bread. I heartily recommend it. It's a good idea to give your dough an hour or two of proving at room temperature before sticking it in there, so that it's at least starting to inflate, and if you do this during the first prove, it will extend the length of your second prove quite a bit. Otherwise, if it's cold outside and you've got somewhere that's down to about 10–12°C (50–54°F) – for example, near a window in a Scottish winter – then you could safely leave a dough overnight there.

4. Stretch and fold

Increase strength by stretching and folding your dough within its bowl once or twice during the first prove. Alternatively, avoid kneading altogether by carrying this out four or more times during the first prove.

If you can't or won't knead, or despite kneading your dough is flopping about all over the place, there could be one of several things going on. The most likely is that your starter isn't active enough. But the other option is that your dough doesn't have enough **strength**. Strength is gained by developing gluten and then shaping it into the right arrangement.

The essential tool in upping your dough strength is stretching and folding. This is such a big deal that most bread books now don't even mention kneading or mixing at all, because this method works so well on its own. I'm often asked how to stop a dough from splatting everywhere following its second prove, and the answer is almost always a few stretches and folds through the first prove. This is especially true if it has been proved cool or cold, as the lack of activity will make your dough weaker.

If you choose to rely on the stretch and fold as your sole method of kneading, then you've got to be around. By that I mean in the house, rather than carrying a bowl around with you and constantly thinking about when it might need another stretch. Personally, I like to mix and forget. Then, if I'm passing through the kitchen, the dough might get a quick fondle. But you should do whatever suits – almost all of my doughs are a hybrid of an initial development with a few stretches and folds through their first prove to enhance strength.

Stretch and fold

1. Wet your fingers with a little water and grab the edge of the dough

2. Stretch it towards you, but not enough so that it tears

3. Gently fold it to the other side of the dough

4. Turn the bowl and repeat, Wetting your fingers if they stick

One particularly effective variant is the **lamination method**. If you're struggling with the technique or despite stretching and folding, your dough still flops everywhere, try this approach. Whichever you choose, try not to add any additional dry flour, as this will interrupt the structure we're trying to create. A lamination step can be very useful if you want to incorporate ingredients into your bread dough – opposite you can see some lemon zest and poppy seeds being sprinkled over a white bread dough.

Lamination

1. On a damp surface, stretch your dough into a big rectangle

2. Evenly scatter any fillings over the dough

3. Fold it over like a letter, so that it is a third of the original size

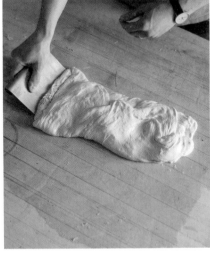

4. Roll your new rectangle up so that it fits back in your bowl

5. Split, pre-shape and shape

Turn your dough out onto an unfloured surface and split it into your desired number of loaves using a scraper. Pre-shape into rough balls and leave them for 20–30 minutes. Form into your final shape and place each loaf in a floured proving basket.

The importance of shaping bread cannot be understated, and it is the most difficult and most technical aspect of bread making to learn. In short, it's annoying.

The problem is this. If you decide to simply chop your proved dough into lengths and roll them into sausage shapes before baking, you won't get something that resembles a baguette (and you'll probably end up with a sticky mess over your hands). If you stick it in a loaf tin without shaping, you'll get bread that's welded into the corners of the tin and with a poor, limp crust. Bake a badly shaped loaf on a baking stone and some bits might burst open, but others will be dense. The crust will be shoddy. And that's if you can even get it out of whatever you've proved it in.

Shaping is important. In sourdough, we often shape in two stages. First, there's the splitting of the dough into however many loaves you're making and **pre-shaping** it (see page 60) – this makes your dough strong. This has to be followed by another rest, called the **bench rest**, preferably of at least 20–30 minutes, to allow your gluten to relax enough to let you shape it again.

Second, there's the final shaping into whichever shape you want your loaf to be. This controls how it rises in the oven and dictates how you're going to score the loaf. If you want those beautiful tears in the surface of your bread, it's got more to do with the shaping than the scoring. I'll take you through the various shapes with some step-by-steps on pages 62–67.

Shaping sourdough is a little different from shaping conventional yeasted breads. It requires more care – you want to be gentle. If it feels like you're having to force your bread into a certain shape, don't. Gently roll and pull until it goes as tight as it wants to, and that's it. And shaping, like kneading, should be done with as little added flour as possible. Splitting and pre-shaping should be done with none, ideally. Anything added now will only interrupt your final structure.

Splitting and pre-shaping

1. Use a scraper to divide the dough into your required number of loaves

2. Wedge your dough scraper underneath a piece of dough

3. Drive your scraper forwards so that the dough catches and curls underneath

4. Turn your scraper 90 degrees around your dough and repeat until smooth

Shaping a boule

1. Scoop your dough onto a floured surface, smooth-side down

2. Stretch one edge of the dough towards you

3. Fold it into the centre

4. Work your way around the dough, repeating this

Shaping a boule (continued)

5. Stop when it feels taut and bouncy

6. Flip your dough over

7. Scoop curved hands under the dough, moving one forwards and one backwards

8. Repeat 3–4 times, until tight and smooth

Shaping a batard (or for loaf tins)

1. Scoop your dough onto a floured surface, smooth-side down

2. Stretch the two sides of the dough away from each other

3. Fold them over each other in the middle

4. Turn the dough by 90 degrees and repeat

Shaping a batard (continued)

5. Now do the same with two corners

6. It should feel very tight

7. From any angle, roll the dough towards you like a Swiss (jelly) roll

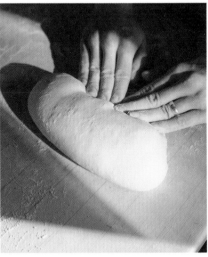

8. Press down at the seam to seal

Shaping and scoring baguettes

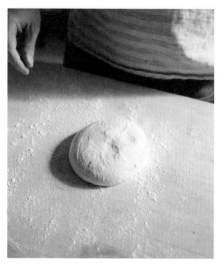

1. Scoop your pre-shaped dough onto a floured surface, smooth side down

2. Fold the bottom third of the dough over, pressing to seal

3. Fold the top third over and seal

4. Keep rolling the top of the dough towards you until it feels tight

Shaping and scoring baguettes (continued)

5. For extra tightness, fold over your seam, sealing with the heel of your hand

6. Gently roll the dough back and forwards underneath your open hands to make it longer

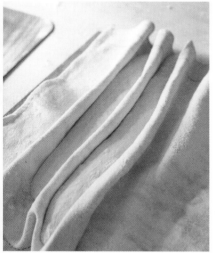

7. Transfer to your floured couche to prove, seam side up

8. Turn onto a dusted peel. Score down their length to the tips, almost parallel to their edges

6. Second prove

Rest your dough for a further 2 hours. Alternatively, you can prove it in the fridge.

The second prove isn't required in every bread. Pizzas and flatbreads, for example, often miss it out, because they rely on the striking heat of the oven and any residual gas to aerate them. But in most breads, this stage is required for lightness and consistency of structure.

The second prove is often shorter – as a rule, half to two thirds of the time. Therefore, I'd suggest proving these loaves for **2 hours** at room temperature. Be wary of this rest – it's a little more sensitive. If your bread becomes overproved during the first, it's no big deal: shape it and prove it again. If your bread is left for too long at this stage, you get very fragile, overinflated bubbles that will burst, if not with the slightest of touches then inevitably as your loaf is slid into the oven. This leads to a denser, stodgier loaf.

Because **bread can be baked just as well straight from the fridge**, retarding this prove allows you to control rather precisely when your bread goes in the oven, as well as adding loads of flavour and further enhancing those big beautiful bubbles. Using the fridge is convenient. Don't have time to finish your sourdough off tonight? No problem – stick it in the fridge and forget about it overnight. Don't have the oven space to bake two at a time? Bake them back to back.

If you decide to fridge, do consider the time it takes for the dough to cool down. It will take a while for the cold to penetrate the centre of the dough. In fact, much of your dough probably has up to 1 hour's close-to-room-temperature proving **after** being placed in the fridge. Thinner loaves cool quicker. And once it is cool, activity doesn't cease: proving in the fridge overnight is roughly equivalent to an extra hour of room-temperature proving. Therefore, if you tuck the dough in the fridge for the night after more than an hour into the second prove, expect a slightly overproved loaf in the morning.

If you're making a loaf in a loaf tin of any sort, the second prove is carried out within the tin itself. This can give it, especially if it's very wet or shaping has been a trial, ample chance to weld itself to your tin. Always heavily grease a loaf tin, right to the corners. Use butter, or some other hard fat. Do not use oil.

If your loaves are to be hand-finished, it's best to prove your dough in a **proving basket.** As discussed earlier, this is a wonderful device that supports the structure of your dough and allows you to slide it into or onto a preheated surface. I cover it in a plastic bag to stop the surface drying out; if the exposed dough is allowed to dry, you'll get a thicker, less tasty quality to the base.

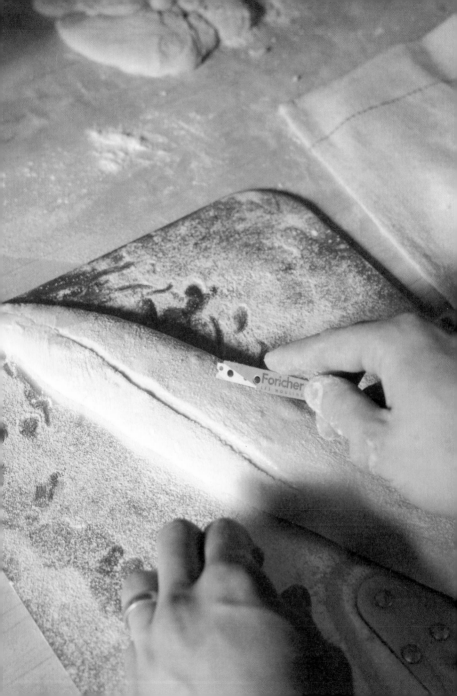

7. Score

Turn your dough onto a semolina-dusted peel (or flat baking sheet) and score using a razor blade or lame.

First, you need to turn your loaf out of your proving basket. We can turn our dough straight onto a peel, or whatever substitute we are using to slide our bread onto our baking surface, or into our pot. Make sure this is well dusted with semolina. If you're baking inside a pot from cold, you can turn your loaf straight out into the pot for scoring.

If your loaf is stuck to the basket, lift it a few centimetres above your tray. Be patient – your loaf will slowly unstick itself. If it was stuck, it's probably about to flop into a large pancake, because loaves usually stick when they're lacking a little in strength. Next time, stretch and fold a few more times, shape a bit tighter or use more flour on your basket. Or all three.

Anyway, I hope you used lots of semolina. Once it's out, give your tray a wiggle back and forth to give the base an even coating and make sure it isn't stuck.

Use a knife, razor blade or lame to score the bread. How you score it will dictate how it rises: your bread will rise in the oven perpendicular to your scores. This can be a hard concept to explain, but the first time you see it, you'll get it. It means that, for example, if you've made a loaf that's perfectly round and you give it one almighty score, your bread will *widen perpendicular to this score in the oven*. This means that a round dough with one score (or several parallel scores) ends up as an oval-shaped loaf. If you want to keep its round shape, you could score with a perfect cross or '+' sign; this means your loaf will open up preferentially on the top of the bread. Or if you score with overlapping lines creating a square, you'll get an even rise all the way across its surface.

You'll figure it out. When scoring, less is more. If you want a rustic gash (called an 'ear') contrasting with totally smooth sides, one gentle cut down the entire length of your *baton* or *batard* will suffice. Scoring it all over with lots of smaller cuts will result in none of these opening up in the same way.

Finally, while we might feel like we have a lot of creative freedom when it comes to scoring, we should always score considering the way the dough has been shaped. Scoring helps to maximise the aeration of the bread.

Because we've introduced tension by shaping, this tension directs how the bread wants to rise. With a perfectly round loaf, it's simple because there is even tension all over. With a baguette, baton or batard, we've intentionally introduced lateral tension down the length of the dough. This means that if we score across the dough, side to side, we aren't doing much to release that tension. A dough scored like this will rise poorly.

If we score down the length of the dough, we release tension in a fairly major way and this allows the bread to expand, which as a knock-on effect releases more tension, and allows for even more expansion. It is in this wonderful situation that you can get truly great rises in the oven, known as oven spring, and those wonderful 'ears' of exploding crust.

8. Bake

Bake each loaf in a very hot preheated oven by sliding your dough into a pot, cloche or Dutch oven, or onto a baking stone. Add steam or bake with the lid or cloche on for 20 minutes before removing the lid and baking for another 20–30 minutes.

You cannot bake a bad dough and make it good. You can bake a good dough badly and make it bad.

Baking is carried out immediately after scoring – don't leave your dough to rest again. This means you'll need to have preheated your oven according to what baking method you're going to use. You should almost always preheat your oven to as hot as it will go – usually about 250°C (480°F)/230°C (450°F) fan/Gas 9 for a domestic oven. Then, when it is time to bake, turn it down to about 220°C (430°F)/200°C (400°F) fan/Gas 7, but this will vary depending on your recipe and your preferences. If your oven has an option to turn its fan to slow or off, use this feature.

The short heat-up times of cast iron (see page 76) is one reason I really like using it, and this has led me away from baking stones. I don't need to guess when the bread is going to be ready and preheat the oven ages before, and then leave it on for another half an hour, wasting energy when the dough isn't quite there. With metal, I can see when the dough is imminently ready and then just turn the oven on.

During baking, there's a big change in the size of your loaf – this rise is called **oven spring**. Lots of things contribute. You might have heard that the warmth of your dough causes your yeast to become more active, producing more CO_2. This is true, but it produces a tiny amount. Once the dough hits just over 40°C (104°F), those yeasts are dead. Yeasts contribute very little to oven spring.

What does happen is that CO_2, which was dissolved within your semi-liquid dough (the same way, though to a lesser extent, that CO_2 is dissolved within a beer or in Coca-Cola), moves out of that dough because it becomes less able to contain it the hotter it is. Some of this gas is lost into the oven, and some makes its way into the bubbles. Wetter doughs can store more CO_2 within the dough itself, which is one of the many reasons why wetter doughs tend to give you larger, more irregular bubbles and can be more forgiving if your rises haven't been as good as you'd hoped for.

As well as this, gases expand as they heat up. There are lots of bubbles already contained within your dough, and the CO_2 within these expands rapidly with the heat of the oven. Add to that all this extra CO_2 from your yeast (minimal) and from your dough (some) and this rise can be dramatic.

The crust can form very quickly, especially in fan ovens, leading to a hard shell through which even the force of the expanding gas cannot break. This is especially common in poorly scored loaves that don't allow the centre of the dough to properly expand. This leads to a loaf that may still be delicious and golden, but will be considerably denser than a well-baked counterpart.

One way of counteracting this is with steam. Moisture is an essential part of the baking process, and without steam the crust dries out too quickly and becomes a greyish brown colour. Think of the difference between burnt sugar and luscious caramel; this is what separates a loaf baked in a dry environment and a wet one.

Of course, if you have steam all through the baking process, a crust will never develop and you'll end up with some large steamed dumplings. This is partly why the technique of baking within pots and cloches has become so widely used – taking the lid off is so easy. You can control the time for which your loaf is steamed, and then remove the lid (or indeed the entire pot) to allow (often astonishing) crusts to form. Baking in a pot is basically the only time I'll use non-stick greaseproof baking paper for a single large loaf, just because it helps when lowering it in.

Most flatbreads, tinned loaves, ciabattas, focaccias and baguettes can't be baked within a pot. Here, you should do your best to add some steam into the oven. When baking with stones, I have a cast-iron griddle pan that sits in the bottom of the oven. When I pop my bread in, I fill the griddle pan with water. Because of the grooves in the pan and how it maintains its heat, the steam is impressive. Furthermore, if your oven has both conventional and fan-assisted options, I'd turn off the fan for 5 minutes to stop your steam being blown off too quickly.

You can also just chuck a glass of water onto the side of the oven and at once close the door to enclose the steam, and I do this if I forget to put the pan in. Sometimes, I'll mist my dough directly using a hand-held sprayer, but this is nowhere near as effective as filling your oven with steam. If you decide to use an old detergent bottle as a DIY sprayer, please make sure it is thoroughly rinsed first. Please.

Oven preheating reference guide

Cast-iron or heavy baking tray	20 minutes
Baking stone	40 minutes +
Cast-iron pot (Dutch oven), preheated	20 minutes, with the pot inside
Cast-iron pot, baking from cold	10 minutes, or as long as your oven takes to heat up
Ceramic cloche	10 minutes, or as long as your oven takes to heat up

9. Cool

Place your loaf on a cooling rack or wooden board. Allow to cool to just-warm before slicing.

This is the smallest, most frustrating and probably most controversial step of the whole process. Cooling. Let your loaf cool properly before even thinking about cutting it.

The reasons for this are many. When it is still very hot, your bread is still soft and setting, and if you squish it down with the pressure of a knife, you're likely to crush and permanently damage the bubbles you've worked so hard to craft.

The second is that, quite simply, it's difficult to cut hot bread; your knife will stick to the soft dough-like centre and you'll get a poor, crushed slice. Yes, you could tear your loaf like the pre-millennial heathens we all are, but then you've got the squishing problem again. Then there's the fact that if you eat a whole loaf of just-out-of-the-oven bread, you're going to end up with a big clump of very dense, poorly digestible starch and protein that's going to make you feel a bit rubbish, if not cause you any true harm.

Instead, wait. Listen for the crust to crack as the softer dough contracts, and think about something else. After at least 30 minutes, but preferably 1 hour, slice. It will be worth the wait.

Your sourdough, because of the acid, alcohol and the salt content, has an extremely good shelf life compared with store-bought bread, and will be quite considerably longer than homemade yeasted breads. It will still be good for toast after a week, and you almost never have to worry about it going mouldy. There's no great secret for storing it – I leave each loaf open to the elements, cut-side down on the chopping board, surrounded by its accompaniments.

You can freeze it, too; par-baked loaves freeze especially well. Par-baking involves cutting the total baking time short: for example, baking in a pot for 20 minutes with a lid on, then a mere 10 minutes with it off. You can then bake your par-baked loaf straight from frozen, straight on the oven shelf, and have the equivalent of a freshly baked loaf of sourdough within 20–25 minutes at 220ºC (430ºF)/200ºC (400ºF) fan/Gas 7.

Novel proving schedules

I thought it might be helpful to include some schedules I regularly use to bake bread around a busy life. Some of these are weekend schedules, some weekday, and all are interchangeable. I start my bread whenever the whim takes me.

The weekend of a nine-to-five week

If you're up by 9am on a day off, you can have very good bread by 5pm if you're not out and about.

9.00am	Weigh ingredients, mix and autolyse
9.30am	Knead for 10 minutes. Prove with a stretch and fold or two
1.30pm	Pre-shape and bench rest
2.00pm	Shape and basket
3.45pm	Preheat oven
4.15pm	Score and bake

Sunday morning bacon sandwiches

A lack of bread on a Saturday doesn't have to mean a lack of bread on a Sunday, if you remember early enough. Nor does it mean missing out on your Saturday.

Saturday

Around lunchtime	Weigh ingredients, mix and autolyse, then knead for 10 minutes and prove with a stretch and fold or two
Around dinner time	Pre-shape, bench rest and shape
	Prove for 90 minutes
	Retard in the fridge

Sunday

Earlier than anyone else	Preheat the oven
	Bake

The work cycle

Colleagues at work most appreciate this one, as you become more and more cajoled into bringing loaves in.

7.00am	With half the recipe's flour and water, make a levain
	Mix the other half together to autolyse
	Leave both at room temperature
6.00pm	Add salt and mix together the levain and the autolyse
	Stretch and fold 4–5 times throughout the evening
9.00pm	Pre-shape, bench rest and shape
	Leave at room temperature
10.30pm	Retard in the fridge
7.00am	Bake before work

Long first prove

This schedule is proof that you don't need to check the temperature of your dough, and that sourdough is forgiving. You can easily prove dough around your busy life.

6.30am	Get up 5 minutes early. Mix the ingredients
	Autolyse
	Use the electric mixer to develop the dough while eating breakfast
	Cover and leave somewhere cool, such as by the window
6.30pm	Get home from work
	Pre-shape, bench rest and shape
	Leave the basket in a warm place (on the heater)
8.00pm	Preheat the oven
8.30pm	Bake

Speed sourdough

Some of the best loaves I've made have been through using a similar method to this one. Because you don't develop much flavour from the fermentation, use more earthy flours or a less frequently fed starter.

6.00pm	Weigh and combine using warm water, autolyse
6.30pm	Mix for 5 minutes
	Stretch and fold three times during the first prove
8.30pm	Divide into small loaves and pre-shape
9.00pm	Bench rest
10.20pm	Preheat stones
11.00pm	Bake

Retarded bulk prove

This is one of my most frequently used schedules. Often, I forget to take the starter out of the fridge in the morning before work, or I don't quite have time to prove and shape before a final overnight prove. Here, you can just stick the half-proven, unshaped dough in the fridge, then the next day you can pre-shape and shape as you normally would. Then you can re-fridge it in the basket for at least another few hours, or until you've got a chance to bake it.

9.00am–1.00pm	Take starter out the fridge; feed with warm water and flour
7.00pm	Once starter has at least doubled, mix all the dough ingredients. Autolyse for 30 minutes
7.30pm	Give the dough a knead if you can. Keep the dough warm. Stretch and fold throughout the evening
10.00pm	Refrigerate the bowl overnight
7.00am	Before work, divide, pre-shape, bench rest and shape. Stick the dough back in the fridge
1.00pm–6.00pm	Bake any time from the middle of the day until the evening

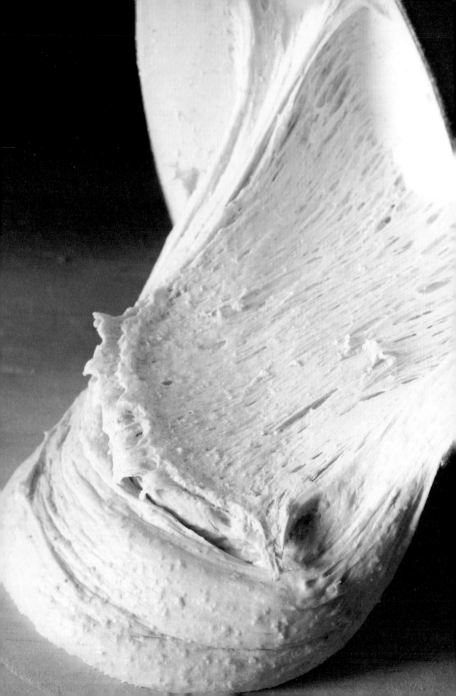

Bread formulae and baker's percentages

This is just a brief word, with the aim of helping you to understand all the mad stuff written online.

Bread formulae are useful as guides to help you compare recipes or scale up to commercial levels, and that's it. I much prefer recipes: this much makes one loaf of this size. Double it or triple it and you'll have three loaves. Simple. The bread formula gives you only the **baker's percentages** of each ingredient, usually set out in a table.

Baker's percentages are calculated based on the total weight of flour in the dough, regardless of its type. Stupidly, they don't include the flour volume contained within your sourdough starter.

As an example, a recipe including

wholemeal flour	100g	33%
rye flour	100g	33%
white flour	100g	33%
Total Flour	**300g**	**100%**
white sourdough starter	**150g**	**50%**
water	**200g**	**66%**

would have a formula of **33% wholemeal, 33% white flour, 33% rye, 50% starter and 66% water**.

The above formula might give the impression of a dough that's 66% hydration, but it isn't. It's actually 73% hydration – this is because the extra flour and water within the sourdough starter mean that the total flour is 375g and the total water is 275g. 275 divided by 375 is 0.73.

This overall number becomes even less relevant when you look at the combination of flours we're using. Who knows what 73% hydration actually means when it comes to this particular mix? All I can tell you is that it will be very stiff. It's easy to compare like-for-like when using a standardised white flour, but not when blending. This is when the whole thing becomes a very rough tool, and sometimes altogether meaningless.

The health and stage of your starter affects the wetness of your dough, too, and thus the dough's subsequent rheology. An over-fermented starter will be wet with broken-down gluten and high acidity. A recently fed starter will combine into your dough much more like flour and water, but might not yet have the number of yeasts required to adequately ferment your dough.

Levain

You'll read, if you wish to, about many people who add in an extra step when making their sourdough. This involves separating the sourdough starter from the dough to create a *levain*.

This is the American perversion of a French term, and is equivalent to a pre-dough or a pre-ferment that is fed from your sourdough starter and then incorporated into your dough. This step will add an extra 6–12 hours to your total proving time, depending on how long you leave this ferment to rise.

I don't use levains because an active sourdough starter does the same job, and in all honesty, my brain can't process an extra step in my bread making.

Starter care:

the secret to consistent sourdough

Keeping your starter happy

There are plenty of reasons your starter can fail, but there are plenty of reasons for it to thrive, too. These are the practical things you can do to aid in keeping it healthy – and keeping you sane – and the things you can change in order to make some seriously awesome bread.

Flour

Sourdough starters can be started and maintained with almost any flour. However, in my humble experience, stoneground, wholemeal, organic flours are the ones that consistently work well. It doesn't matter whether it's rye, spelt or wholemeal, just make sure the whole meal is in it. This maximises the available bugs.

Many recipes, though, call for a white sourdough starter. This doesn't mean your starter must have been started with white flour, but you could go down this route if you want. I hope it works. You can use posh organic white flour to maximise the possibilities of success.

I used to have several starters going at once, but it was a faff. Now, I keep whatever starter I have going, and occasionally transition it from white to wholemeal to rye and back or any which way. If I run out of a certain sort of flour, I'll feed it with whatever I've got in the cupboard.

If I've got a rye starter on the go and want to make a white bread, I have a few options. Most often, I just use my rye starter and adjust the recipe accordingly. Sometimes, I'll dilute however much starter I need with water and drain this liquid through a fine sieve or tea strainer to remove the bran. But if I really want the sinfully white nature of the bread, I'll sift out the bran in the same way, and mix the resulting starter-y water with white flour in a new container. By the next day, I'll have a fully active and ready-to-use white starter.

When you change your starter to a white one, the changes you notice can be quite profound – the activity will be less. Wholemeal and rye starters are very active because they have so much more available sugar for the yeast to grow, and possibly because (though I have no way of knowing for sure) you're adding so many more bugs in on top of the existing ones each time.

The acidity levels in your white starter will be higher. Some people find that their complexity is higher, too. I don't know how you'd test for this.

Starter storage

Basically, anything. My vessel of choice when experimenting with loads of different variations of starter was a 100ml (3½fl oz) tumbler, of which I have many. They were easy to clean and I could standardise my experiments. I laid cling film (plastic wrap) on top to keep the starter moist.

I'm not suggesting you do this. I'm simply making the point that you don't need anything special, and you don't need very much flour either. All of these successful starters were kicked off with less than a tablespoon of flour. I've heard famous bakers say that the more flour you use, the better – and that's kind of true. But you don't want to be dumping more starter than you need to.

If you're making one loaf at a time, then a simple jam (jelly) jar or Kilner (Mason) jar is excellent. Washed, obviously, this holds about 200g of active starter, at a push, which is plenty. Keep 50–100g of starter back and feed with 50g each of flour and water every time. I use this for times of relative inactivity. I wouldn't screw the lid on – you can get a good seal with a jam jar, and it will explode if you do this. Just lay the lid gently on top to stop the starter drying out.

For more loaves, I'd go with a glass clip-top jar, but with the rubber seal removed. Again, this avoids the explosion or cracking risk from too much pressure. Using glass jars is handy, because you can monitor the aeration (and thus the stage following feeding) of your starter and keep an eye on its health.

Less good (but still good) is the plastic lunchbox or Tupperware box. They're great for even larger volumes of dough, with an eliminated risk of glass breakages, but they also stop you from seeing what's going on inside.

Unless you've got transparent plastic. That would solve the problem.

Because I'm the most indulgent hipster bread baker of them all, I keep my starter in a hand-thrown ceramic fermentation jar.

Temperature

The basic choice when it comes to temperature is whether to store your starter in the fridge or at room temperature. I would never store a starter hotter than room temperature because of how quickly you'll burn through the feeds. And if your temperature isn't controlled, you could risk going hot enough to kill your yeast.

Start your starter at whatever your room temperature is, and so long as it is somewhere between 16–28°C (61–82°F), it will be fine. There will be variations in how quickly it takes to get going, but your starter will get going at some point.

Storing is different. If you are storing your starter at room temperature, you have the potential to keep it very active. However, most home starters I know that are kept in this way, like mine was for many years, aren't in great health.

You should be (at least) doubling the weight of your starter every time you feed it. As an example, a starter that weighs 100g should be fed with at least 50g flour and 50g water. If you don't use it and keep it out of the fridge, you'll either have to pour away some starter or double the starter size again, this time using 100g flour and 100g water. If you let this get out of hand, it can mean a loaf's worth of starter every day is wasted.

People compensate for this by not feeding their starters properly, or less frequently. I'm guilty of this. It means you get a lot of *hooch* (that liquid that sits on the top), poor activity, unhealthy yeast and ultimately dense, slack bread made from unmanageably sloppy doughs.

So my advice is to keep your starter in the fridge. Don't convince yourself that you're going to bake sourdough every day (unless, of course, you do). If you give it a feed once the majority has been used to make dough, and you leave it out as you prove, you'll have a starter that's beginning to bubble and grow at the same time as your loaf.

cont.

This can actually be really useful for tracking the progress of your loaf.

Then stick it in the fridge, after 4–6 hours or so, and it will cool down gradually. Its remaining fermentation will be very slow. As soon as you take it back out of the fridge and it's warmed up again, it's ready to use. This method works whether it's a week or two days between bakes.

Stiff versus sloppy

There's a lot of debate in the technological bread-o-sphere about whether it is best to store your sourdough starter stiff – usually about 50% hydration (1 part water to 2 parts flour) – or sloppy, at 100% hydration as I generally recommend (equal parts).

The truth is that it doesn't make that much difference. Stiff starters can be quite practical for big bakeries, because you can chop off pieces of them and weigh them, and you've got big machines that are able to mix it all up easily. Sloppy starters are great for the home because they are very easy to mix in, and you can store them in anything that can hold a liquid.

The differences shouldn't be much, so long as the stiff starter has been properly combined. If there are large areas within your stiff starter that contain only flour and water, and you've not got much starter mixed in here, your bugs will need to migrate into this quite solid structure, therefore negotiating a slightly more complex matrix. For this reason, stiff starters are often said to be slower growing and less acidic. Because they seemingly last longer, lots of people advocate keeping them in the fridge if you bake sourdough less frequently.

I don't see much evidence for any profound effects on the dough either way. I use sloppy because it's easy. I would go with whatever you prefer and adjust the recipes with more or less water accordingly.

Drying and freezing

I often get messages on social media asking about drying or freezing a starter in order to keep it for a long period of time. Neither is perfect, nor would I really advocate either. It's pretty easy to start a new one from scratch. If you are getting good bread with a particular starter, the reality is that it probably has little to do with the starter itself.

I've seen guides for drying starters involving spreading them thinly and then putting them in the oven on a low heat. This beggars belief – temperatures over 50°C (122°F) will kill the vast majority of bugs in your starter. The dried flakes might add the necessary acid to get a new starter going, but there will be little left of the old.

If you would like to dry your starter, spread a few tablespoons very thinly over a sheet of non-stick greaseproof baking paper. Leave it at room temperature to dry naturally – it will take at least a day. It should then splinter and break apart quite easily. You can store this in a jar in the fridge for… I don't really know how long. Quite a few bugs will probably still be there years later.

And as for freezing, just don't. Some yeasts, in a solution of flour, do survive the freezing process. *Some*. Many will die. Seriously, don't bother freezing your starter.

Starter troubleshooting

'My starter has separated into a liquid layer and a floury layer'
Try not to think of it as separation – rather, think of it as the more solid parts of your mixture settling to the bottom.

All starters settle. This is a natural process that happens as time passes. Once your yeast and bacteria have finished dissecting and then munching through your flour's starch, they slow down and relax. As they do, they stop churning up the starter, and because they've also broken down many of your proteins, the delicate structure collapses. The liquid at the top is a mixture of water, alcohol and acid, as well as plenty more bugs and some protein. Or really bad sour wheat beer, if you will. The slang name for this stuff is *hooch*.

If your starter had been bubbling plenty beforehand, take settling as a sign that the yeasts have exhausted their food source and the starter needs feeding. If you're often getting separation, it could mean a few different things – the most likely is that you aren't feeding your starter often enough to maintain good yeast activity, or that you need to feed it with more flour and water. You want to at least double the weight of your starter every time you feed it. And if you aren't going to feed it to double its weight again the next day, stick it in the fridge.

The other common cause of hooch is a starter that's been brought to the brink of death through neglect, and then an attempt has been made to revive it. In this instance, despite many feeds, it hardly bubbles and then separates. Here, your balance of yeast and bacteria is wrongly skewed towards the latter. You can either pour most of it away and try re-dosing it with rye or wholemeal flour, or you can start again.

'My starter hasn't started'
If you get no activity from your starter at all, there are a few possibilities.

If you get a separation (rather like the above) from the start without any bubbles, you've been successful in culturing lactic acid bacteria (most likely) and little else. You haven't created the wonderful synchronicity between the bugs required.

cont.

The most likely issue here is that you've used the wrong flour. Use good wholemeal, preferably rye, organic flour; try adding some fruit juice.

If you get no bubbles at all, and it still smells floury after a week or more, then I'd be willing to bet that your starter is too cold. Stick it near to the heater, but not on it. It simply isn't the case that your flour is sterile – there's always something in it, and likely millions of things. Just occasionally, there are far fewer than you'd like, or the wrong organism. If in doubt, add some more flour; the dirtier and fresher flour, the better.

'My starter is black, red or blue'

Moulds are beautiful, colourful things. Their growth is relatively uncommon in a developed, active starter. They're in it, and on it, but they're stamped down by the overwhelming fermentation that dominates, and that you use in the creation of your bread.

You can start to get mould growth from as little as three days after a starter has separated (see above). The most common is a black mould, which is usually (but not always) of the *Aspergillus* species. This isn't harmful to humans, apart from those who are very unwell with diseases that attack their immune system, though I don't know what ingesting a black sourdough starter raw would do to even the healthiest of people. Probably bad things.

If you're determined to save your beloved starter (please don't be), then you can pour away the black stuff and give it a feed with some good flour. If it bubbles within a couple of days, great. If it doesn't, don't lose any sleep. Start again.

Blue or white fluffy moulds are a similar story – they grow in the presence of oxygen and are strongly inhibited by alcohol, so it normally takes quite a lengthy period of neglect for them to grow, usually on the drier bits of flour that line the sides of your starter receptacle. This is fine – just scrape them out and don't neglect your starter so much in future.

Bright pink, orange or reddish moulds tend to be the nastier ones, and might not be moulds at all, but rather bacteria. Pink examples are *T. thermophilus* (a cool, heat-tolerant organism), *E. coli* (some strains harmful, some not) and certain *Lactobacillus* strains. Starters are melting pots of interesting bugs, and you don't know what's going to happen when your fermentation settles down.

Pink moulds are more associated with producing toxins that are harmful to humans, and these toxins (called *mycotoxins*) survive the baking process. I've never heard or read of anyone becoming unwell ever, ever, ever through eating cooked sourdough. And I've checked. But I'm legally and ethically bound to suggest that if your starter has a neon mould of any such colour, then you should chuck it out and have a shower.

'My starter doesn't rise and fall – it's lethargic'

You want your starter, following feeding and mixing, to rise dramatically. Quite what volume it reaches will depend on the dimensions of your container, but it should double or triple in size following a feed and be filled with loads of tiny bubbles.

If your bubbles are numerous but not evenly distributed, and your starter seems to take ages to get going, you needn't worry. It's perfectly healthy, but it's just not mixed in well enough. You should incorporate your new flour and water until you've got a smooth, consistent dough.

Despite this, if you're still not getting the rise, then try a period of keeping the starter out of the fridge and being really strict with feeding it every day. If, even then, you're still not getting a rise, consider the temperature as a factor. You should warm it up to see whether that helps.

Finally, if your starter is white, try adding some stoneground wholemeal or rye into the mix, as well as increasing the ratio of new flour and water to old starter. A few daily feeds and it will likely get going.

Bread trouble-shooting

These are all relative terms. Your bread is probably awesome and you're nit-picking. If your bread really, really isn't awesome, don't despair. Let's fix it for next time. I'm sorry if your particular quandary doesn't appear: this list isn't exhaustive, but it covers most of the common 'flaws'.

If you are of the mindset that bread doesn't have flaws and instead each loaf is a manifestation of the baker's individual creative freedom, regardless of their results, good for you. Skip past this chapter. I am envious.

'My bread is dense'

Dense doughs are most commonly caused by starter woes. Most likely, your starter could be in a poor condition. If in doubt, take it out of the fridge and feed it daily or even twice daily, pouring away the excess starter.

If your starter is fine, it means your bread is underproved. This means it hasn't been given enough time, or the temperature of your dough was too low. Try using warmer water and proving somewhere warm, especially during the first prove. This will also aid the structure of your dough – your gas-filled, acidic dough will have very good strength.

Sometimes, an overproved dough can be dense. Time and *Lactobacillus* bacteria will break down protein, and that causes your dough to slop and its air-capturing ability to be diminished. Otherwise, overproving can cause your gluten to be overstretched and the delicate matrix to collapse when the dough is moved to the oven. This is more common in doughs that are a little underdeveloped and need a bit more stretching and folding for the amount of moisture they have.

'My dough hasn't risen at all'

If it appears that your dough hasn't risen, then I'd encourage you still to shape it and bake it, then see what happens. I feel a lot of these complaints are made about doughs that are subsequently thrown away. You just don't know – your second prove might take off, especially with a bit of heat. Following baking, you might find a massive expansion and perfectly adequate aeration. If not, examine the crumb structure. If it's dense, see the previous point about dense loaves. It's probably your starter.

'My sourdough is too sour'

This is also usually an issue with the starter. Some starters, especially those fed infrequently and kept at room temperature, can be very sour. This causes a slow or delayed rise, a flat, floppy dough and a very tangy, chewy crumb. If this is you, work on your starter activity levels, and keep it in the fridge when not in use.

It can be that you've got a very active starter, and it's being used too late in the cycle of feeding – if you leave it for more than 24 hours since the last feed, or more than a week in the fridge, often the acid will dominate. Try to use your active starter at peak volume, 8–14 hours after feeding. If you have a penchant for a very sour loaf, you could try leaving your starter for longer than 24 hours before using it.

While rye flour is a little more sour than wheat flour, a wholemeal or rye starter tends to produce much less tangy loaves. Yeast populations and sugar availability are much higher in these starters, so they tend to ferment faster and cleaner.

'My dough flops or spreads before baking'

This is the big one – I get more questions about this than any other flaw. Your dough isn't strong enough.

The simplest way to increase strength is to reduce the amount of liquid in your dough. This is fine when you're starting off, but it will give you a slightly denser bread with a crumb that isn't so soft.

Assuming the recipe is good, the most common reason for a lack of strength in colder-climate countries is a less-than-vigorous fermentation. You want your yeast to produce carbon dioxide at a high enough rate to keep inflating your bubbles. This gives the dough lots of strength.

Therefore, a poor starter is commonly to blame – follow the entire section on starter troubleshooting. If you're sure it isn't that, try increasing the temperature of your water and proving in a warm place – aim for the dough to be about 25°C (77°F).

At this point, if your fermentation is fine and you're still getting sloppy dough, it's either to do with the development of your gluten, or a lack of tightness when shaping. The first often leads to the second.

Gluten could be developed further by kneading for longer at the beginning, but if you overdevelop at this stage, your gluten can become too tight. Compromise and add some stretches and folds during the first prove. Two or three, spaced out, following an initial (but modest) mix is usually enough to sort out your dough strength.

If you're not in the habit of dividing and pre-shaping your wet doughs, get into it. It's pretty much essential for maintaining enough strength to get a decent shape.

Finally, a sloppy dough could be the shaping itself – make sure you've got light fingers, work quickly and use floured hands to stop them sticking. You don't want to bash and squeeze the gas out of the dough as many traditional French or English bakers might – it's a delicate process.

'The dough's too wet to work with'

First, check the recipe. Make sure that you weighed all the correct ingredients with accuracy. Check your scales. Does a pack of butter weigh the amount stated, or a 1kg bag of sugar actually weigh exactly that?

If so, it's probably a situation that's similar to my last point on sloppy doughs. Wetness is usually a result of poor dough strength. If you're starting out, the easiest way to increase dough strength is to add flour, and that's fine. Just add a little and feel how the dough develops – but try not to add quite as much the next time.

A dough that is stretched and folded during its first prove following a decent knead will feel completely different to a dough that's left without fondling. Temperature is also an important factor. Doughs that rise quickly will maintain more strength, whereas the bacteria that prosper in the cold will break down the proteins in the dough to give you an even floppier, wetter-feeling dough.

'My dough deflates when handled or scored'

Deflation happens when the dough has been overproved. The gluten structure is overly stretched to precarious levels, and so it will collapse with the slightest provocation. You'll say goodbye to all that aeration you've been waiting for. I'd still bake your loaf, because many of these burst bubbles will

fill back up again during the time in the oven. You'll just notice your crumb is a little close, with lots of middling, thick-walled bubbles.

Rest for less time following shaping, or reduce the temperature. The cold helps with the gluten's stability, so a cold and overproved loaf is more stable than a warm one, which tends to splat. That's partly why proving in the fridge is a relatively safe thing to do.

If your shaped dough is already overproved and you've forgotten to preheat your oven, get it in the fridge as soon as you realise. If the dough looks particularly swollen and unstable, I wouldn't bother scoring, as the cuts won't open up and you'll just end up deflating things further.

'My crust is pale, thick and tough'

A thick crust may be because your bread has been baked for quite a long time. I don't mind this, and from time to time that's what I'm after. But a thick, tough, tooth-breaking crust isn't a good thing. There are quite a few possible causes.

The first is poor or non-existent shaping – this appears in loaves baked in tins or if made in bread makers, as some people assume you don't need to shape. Not only does the dough weld itself to the sides, but the top is thick and dense. What makes a good crust are the layered sheets of gluten, aligned parallel to the crust. Fail to achieve this and the crust becomes craggy, bubbly and altogether poor.

The other reason for a thick, unpleasant crust is inadequate caramelisation. This could be because it has been underproved, but it is usually because there's not enough moisture when baking: either your proving dough has been left open to the elements and developed a dry, leathery skin on it, or you've not added enough steam at the beginning of your bake. A fan oven can really dry out loaves, so you need to be careful to add extra steam. To test whether it's this, bake your loaf in a pot with the lid on for the first 20 minutes and see what happens.

'My loaves burn easily'

This is an interesting one. The first thing to check is your oven temperature – obviously, this means making sure you're setting it to the right temperature.

If necessary, buy an oven thermometer. All ovens have cold and warm spots, even efficient fan ovens. But you should put it roughly in the centre of your oven, and ensure that it is what it says it should be in that spot. Adjust as necessary.

If it's not that, it could be your loaves. Overproving during the first prove, especially a cold and very long one, can cause an overabundance of sugars. These are more likely to burn. I like that burnt sugar look and taste, though – it might be that you need to adjust what you define as 'burnt' and what you see as 'caramelised'.

'My crumb is raw or doughy in the centre'

A raw crumb happens when there's a mismatch between your loaf looking cooked but still not being baked in the middle. The solution is to turn down your oven and bake for a bit longer. It helps to check the true temperature of your oven using an oven thermometer, as above.

Sometimes doughiness can be caused by other things: often too much sugar added to your dough will cause your crumb to be overly wet and dense. I've seen this if I've gone a wee bit overboard in how much honey I'm adding to a walnut loaf. The same has happened in brioches, where I've experimented by adding lots of sugar. This gives the texture of a sweaty insole.

'I don't have lots of huge bubbles'

You've done well. You're making sourdough, it's working out. But the crumb doesn't have that huge, open structure that you've seen from the very best.

There's no one answer to this question. Big, irregular bubbles are things that commercial bakers have been trying to eliminate for hundreds of years because it isn't particularly practical to spread and butter. But now they're a sign of good sourdough, for stupid reasons, and people want to emulate them. Follow the steps in this book and you should achieve them. The key points are summarised below:

- An active starter, above all
- A high-hydration dough
- An autolyse, without salt

- A modest initial mix
- A warm, active first prove with two or three stretches and folds
- Gentle pre-shaping and shaping
- A very steamy bake, such as inside a lidded pot or a Dutch oven

'My loaf has irregular oven spring or random growths'

Oven spring is largely due to the carbon dioxide in your dough filling the bubbles and then expanding them rapidly. If this is going on while the crust has already formed, it tends to expand along the lines of your scores. The bubbles expand along the path of least resistance. Therefore, if the majority of your crust has formed but a cold spot means that one bit hasn't quite yet, your bubbles will expand this way. This can lead to 'growths' on the side of your bread where the dough has broken through.

You can stop this by scoring as per my guide on page 71 – shallow but decisive and along the lines of the dough's shaping. Plenty of steam will delay crust formation and allow the loaf to expand properly. Finally, don't bake your loaves too close together, or you'll create uneven crust formation and, consequently, irregularity will be inevitable.

'My scores don't open up'

Like any of these problems, there's no single solution.

The most common reason for this is shaping that is not quite adequate, which in itself is often caused by a dough that isn't strong enough to begin with. If you haven't created adequate tension in the dough, it won't burst open. Practise your shaping, and give it a pre-shape.

It goes without saying that you need to have proved your bread properly for it to burst open – those bubbles have to be contained within the dough in order for them to expand. If there aren't any bubbles, you'll have a dense brick of a loaf.

Conversely, if your dough has too much gluten development and not enough yeast activity to expand your bubbles (for example, during a long, cold first prove), you'll have a solid dough with very thick-walled bubbles. The pressure required to overcome the force of the gluten is quite huge, and so you won't reach your potential expansion in the oven.

If your dough is a little overproved during the second prove and your bubbles have reached the maximum size they possibly can, your scores won't open. A relatively lightly proved dough, following an adequate or extended first prove, has the potential for massive expansion in the oven if scored properly. This is why baguettes are have such impressive 'ears' (see page 131).

'I've got a line of dense dough at the bottom (or at the side) of tins'

Inherently there's a risk that proving in tins (or even proving the loaf the same way up as it's going to bake) is going to cause an irregularity in your crumb, with dense dough and smaller bubbles towards the bottom, and big bubbles that open up at the top.

Usually, and as is the case with many problems, this is made more likely by inadequate dough strength or shaping that needs a bit more tightness. If you dump your loaf in the tin without shaping, it's going to have a flat, dense bottom because you've not developed a structure that can support it. When stretching and folding, make sure the dough is shaped a little tighter.

Then, the only thing you've got to do is make sure not to overprove it; once the gluten is stretched to that extent, the structure will fail and you'll end up with a line of stodge wherever the dough was in contact with the tin.

'There are massive bubbles or tunnels through the loaf, or under the crust'

There are a few reasons for this. I've often seen it in a loaf that's had a too-cold or underactive first prove – you might notice this happening to loaves as you move into the winter months. Get the prove a little warmer, or pitch a more active starter.

I've also seen it in loaves that have been well developed but then overproved during the second prove. If your loaf was impressively swollen before baking, then it's a sign it was overproved. As you move it about and score it, fragile bubbles might burst and consolidate into one large hole.

Another possible reason for this is that your dough had very poor strength. Add some stretches and folds during the first prove, pre-shape and then shape.

Core recipes

Pain de mie au levain (page 118)

This recipe works to fill a notable void. The bread is complex in flavour and long-lasting, but soft-crumbed and light. Your sourdough doesn't have to be chewy and crusty. *Pain de mie* is a derogatory term in some French bakeries, describing a soft supermarket-style loaf that comes ready-wrapped in plastic. Some artisans never lost the wonderful art of making a good one, and a few others have reclaimed its virtue. It's the everyday bread: *mie* means crumb, and so this bread is about maximising your soft crumb.

San Francisco white sourdough (page 121)

It is hard to define 'San Francisco sourdough' – but I'll try. The classic breads have similar properties: they're made with refined and very strong white American and Canadian flours. The starters are refreshed without quite the same regularity or volume of those across the Atlantic, and as a result, they're more acidic. This acidity is then accentuated with a long and cool prove.

This results in a well-fermented bread with a rich golden crust. The tang is very apparent. The crumb is soft and custardy, and it has the characteristic irregular and large bubbles. It's what people think of when they think 'sourdough'. And here I'll show you how to make a loaf.

Danish rye (page 124)

This is a loaf I don't make nearly enough – then when I do, I'm reminded of its awesomeness and immediately bake it again in a big batch, slice it, wrap it and freeze it. It withstands the freezing process particularly well, maintaining moisture for ever. You can then just stick one slice at a time straight into the toaster and always have access to posh toast or Danish open sandwiches (*smørrebrød*). You don't need an active sourdough starter for this one and it's a great way to use up discarded starter in the fridge.

Brioche (page 127)

Here's a naturally leavened, well-fired brioche for you. To hit the right spot in terms of flavour and acidity, one of your fermentations needs to be long and cool (but not too cold), and I'd make it your first one, if possible. This makes shaping easier. You'll need to get the heat cranked up during the second prove. If you want the best burger buns, follow the recipe but divide your dough into twelve rolls, and bake over two baking trays.

My brioche formula is quite simple and quite easy remember, for those who like bread formulae (see page 83): 100% flour, 50% egg, 40% butter, 40% starter, 30% milk, 10% sugar and 2% salt.

Demi-baguettes à l'ancienne (page 130)

I was going to call this recipe 'baguettes', but I didn't want to upset more people than I had to. Truly, it is difficult to make an authentic baguette at home simply because of the size of domestic ovens. These half-baguettes, made wholly with sourdough, are awesome things.

They are perfect for par-baking and throwing in the freezer – just cut the bake short by 10 minutes. That way, you can get all the hard work out of the way and always have bread available within 15 minutes, cooked straight from frozen.

Your choice of flour for baguettes is important. Don't use stronger Canadian or American flour (usually called 'very strong' flour). This is quite a dry dough in comparison to most in the book – a very strong flour will make the dough too elastic, and you won't get the classic 'ear' forming on each cut as they expand. Any standard strong flour will do, but ideally you want good British flour from a local mill. Yes, British: I've had the best results with local unbleached varieties.

You can get French baguette flour online or from a load of specialist shops. The French flour system is a little confusing – but if you go for T65 flour, then this is about the right level of extraction and milling for baguettes. The '65' refers to the mineral content in the flour (usually about 0.65%) and equates to its level of refinement.

You'll want a couche to complete this recipe – this is a stiff linen cloth that you dust with flour and then use to line up all the baguettes. It allows the baguettes to survive their long, flavour-inducing second prove without spreading too much. If you don't have a couche, you can use a heavy tea towel.

Focaccia integrale (page 135)

To those who feel that the principle of this recipe is an abomination, I implore you to try it.

Integrale means wholemeal. My version of this Italian flatbread is made with good British flour and a decent portion of wholewheat or rye flour – for ease, we'll use whichever makes up your starter. While the focaccia is indeed an ancient bread, the idea that it must only be made with white flour is modern – flours have never been as refined as they are today, and we are hopefully beginning to revolt against this.

This is a recipe for you to play with. The dough is soft and forgiving, and you can incorporate loads of things into it: nuts, chopped olives, onions, garlic or sundried tomatoes all work well. The high oil content helps give it a crumb structure that is rather eccentric and uneven, as it interrupts your gluten – that's why we add it after the mixing. Further oil doused over the top is essential.

Some would say use cheap oil for inside and expensive oil on top. Instead, just use the best oil, all the time. Buy it in bulk if you can, directly from the producers in France, Italy, Spain or Greece. Each country has its own varieties and terroirs, and each will make a different focaccia – this is also part of the fun.

Neapolitan-style pizza (page 140)

I'm not Italian. I've never even been to Naples. And because of that, I don't buy that this can't therefore be the best pizza recipe you'll ever try. It might *not* be, but it doesn't mean it *can't* be.

I'm very fortunate to have a truly excellent Neapolitan pizza place just a few minutes' walk from my house. They utilise a very hot wood-fired oven to bake pizzas in 90 seconds or less, and you're often served their smoking, speckle-crusted pies with slightly soggy centres before the drinks have even come, with a side order of nonchalance.

I've tried lots of ways of recreating the intense, dry heat of a wood-fired oven at home. I even built a wood-fired oven out of a barrel that I chopped in two using an angle grinder. If you want to try it, just sit a cut barrel on some slabs of granite and build an arc of bricks around the entrance using fire cement, *et voilà*. Pizza oven.

While the outdoor pizza is good for parties and summer, Glasgow doesn't have much summer, and in truth, I don't throw many parties. Step forwards, then, the 'skillet-broiler' method, and its variations. This is basically when you use your hob to get a cast-iron frying pan very hot, build your pizza on top of this and then finish it off under the grill to melt the cheese and char the crust. The issue with this is that it doesn't heat the bottom and top together, reducing oven spring potential. It doesn't give you much time to add toppings before burning the base either.

I compromise by getting a cast-iron surface really, really hot over my largest gas burner, while I build up my pizza on a semolina-dusted peel. The thick cast iron holds plenty of heat to cook the pizza. When the pizza is ready to go, I slide it onto the pan and stick it straight under the grill, which has been preheating equally hot. After you've cooked the first pizza, you'll see whether or not you need to spend a bit of time on the hob to crisp the base a little more.

Pretzels (page 145)

Pretzels are my second-favourite bar snack. Sprinkled with good sea salt, they are the perfect accompaniment to a pint of lager – I'm right into the maltiness of *helles*, a robust lager from Munich, but they would equally work well with a crisp, dry *pilsner*. In fact, any lager will do, so long as it abides by the *Reinheitsgebot* (German beer purity law).

In order to obtain the beautiful dark brown shine required of a pretzel, you soak your dough in an alkaline substance prior to baking: this vastly increases the speed of the Maillard reaction (browning reaction between proteins and sugars). You should then bake fast and hard for a deep-brown crust that remains flimsily thin.

Your choice of alkaline substance is difficult. Please be careful if you use the traditional chemical: lye (caustic soda, or sodium hydroxide). Wear rubber gloves and goggles – this stuff is truly life-ruining if mishandled. It will blind you if it gets in your eyes. It will burn your skin. It will kill you, and kill you quite horrifically, if you or someone else accidentally ingests it. But if you want the best pretzels, then you'll need to use this. It is also the best drain cleaner imaginable in its pure form.

If that scares you, then you can make a less dangerous alternative by baking some bicarbonate of soda (baking soda) in the oven: the heat causes the conversion of sodium bicarbonate to sodium carbonate. This releases some CO_2, which can help make cakes or scones rise. Unfortunately, when there is too much sodium carbonate, cakes, scones or soda bread taste too 'bicarby'; that's why we use baking powder, which contains a combination of sodium bicarbonate and tartaric acid. The reaction between the two creates CO_2 without soapiness.

Baked bicarb (I should call it carb, really) is also quite alkaline, much more so than plain bicarb. It should still be handled carefully, but isn't quite so scary as lye. For the chemists: a 5% solution of caustic soda has a pH of >14. A solution of 5% sodium carbonate has a pH of 11.5. Because pH is a logarithmic scale, that means the caustic soda is at least 316 times more alkaline than the sodium carbonate. And therefore 316 times more burn-y. Practically, this means you'll need much longer exposure to the latter for anything close to a half-decent crust.

Crispbread (page 149)

These are sourdough crackers – extra-thin versions of **knäckebröd** or crispbreads. In Scandinavia, they were considered a very humble food for generations past. Now, they're about a fiver for a wee box at the supermarket.

You can top these crackers with anything you like. I particularly like germ (wheatgerm) – the fatty, yolk-equivalent of the wheat seed. Because of its moisture and its fat content, it doesn't stay fresh long. Keep it in the fridge, and try to order it directly from your supplier. You can use anything: seeds are especially nice, pressed in just before baking.

But back to the dough. Any sourdough can be used to create crispbread, so long as it is rolled thinly enough and pricked to prevent puffing. Having a good portion of the flour as wholemeal (wholewheat) or rye helps the eventual cracker crumble and crack. In this case, getting the dough thin enough can be tricky: you can stretch, rest and roll using a rolling pin.

I don't knead this dough – instead, I do a very long autolyse to increase extensibility. Then, rather than stretch and fold, I leave the dough to bulk ferment for as long as possible at as low a temperature as possible. This creates a sticky dough, but one that can be stretched very thin. Use plenty of flour and you'll be fine.

Pain de mie au levain

For 1 large or 2 small pains de mie:
150g white sourdough starter
425g strong white flour, plus extra for dusting
10g table salt
225g tepid-warm water
50g slightly warmed milk
40g unsalted butter, softened, plus extra for greasing

Start by making sure your starter is active. If in doubt, keep it out of the fridge, double the starter in weight and wait 8–12 hours before beginning.

In a large bowl, weigh your flour and then weigh your salt on top. Rub this in so that it is mostly combined. Then, add your water, starter and warm milk on top and mix everything together until roughly combined. Leave to rest for 20–30 minutes before continuing.

Add your butter, and then knead your bread properly until it's silky smooth and stretchy, and it's no longer sticking to your hands or the sides of the bowl. Any kneading method will do, including in a mixer.

Cover your bowl and leave your dough somewhere warm – close to (but not on) a radiator will do. You want it warmer than room temperature, about 25°C (77°F) if possible. Wrap it in a couple of tea towels to insulate it.

After 3–4 hours, it should have risen quite substantially. You should now scrape it from its bowl, being careful to maintain its delicate structure, and onto your unfloured work surface. Use a dough scraper to pre-shape (see page 60) your dough into rough boules and leave them for 20–30 minutes. Meanwhile, grease as many loaf tins (either one 900g/2lb tin or two 450g/1lb tins) as you need with plenty of butter.

After your bench rest, lightly flour your surface and flip your dough onto the dusting. Shape it gently into a batard shape (see pages 64–5) and then gently transfer it to your tin. Place your tin inside a plastic bag and leave it at room temperature for about 2–2½ hours, or until notably huge. Alternatively, you can retard your bread in the fridge from about an hour into this prove.

I like to stone bake my loaves, so I preheat my oven to 250ºC (480ºF)/ 230ºC (450ºF) fan/Gas 9 at least 30–40 minutes before I'm expecting my loaf to be ready. If you're not using a stone, 10 minutes will do. When your dough has risen by at least one and a half times, remove it from the plastic bag and stick it in the oven. Add plenty of steam, and turn your oven down to 220ºC (430ºF)/200ºC (400ºF) fan/Gas 7. Bake for 35–40 minutes for one large loaf, or until golden brown on top.

Remove your tin from the oven and bash out your loaf onto your work surface – it should come out easily. Place the bread back in the oven for 5–10 minutes for slightly crustier sides. If you'd prefer not, leave it where it is and enjoy the thin, delicate crust. Cool for at least an hour before slicing, however hard that may be.

San Francisco white sourdough

For 1 large loaf:
425g very strong white flour, plus extra for dusting
150g white sourdough starter, 18–30 hours following its last feed
300g tepid water
10g table salt
semolina, for dusting

In a large bowl, weigh your flour, starter and tepid water. Mix these together with a dough hook or wooden spoon and let them sit for 30–60 minutes – otherwise known as the autolyse.

Following this, add your salt (don't forget!) and hand knead for about 5 minutes or so, or until the dough feΔels smooth and supple in your hands. I'd use the slap and fold method (see pages 50–51), as this gives the dough some strength. Alternatively, you could mix in a stand mixer at low–medium speed (speed '2' usually) for about 5 minutes.

Cover your bowl with a plate or tea towel and let it sit in a relatively warm place – near a heater is fine. You want to leave it for 4 hours or so. During this time, I'd give it at least two or three stretches and folds (see page 55) to imbue strength.

Once your dough is suitably airy and maintaining its shape between folds, scrape your dough out onto an unfloured work surface. Use a scraper to pre-shape the loaf by driving your scraper underneath to tighten it (see page 60). Bench rest for 30 minutes.

If your loaf has spread out significantly (into a flat, pancake-like mound), it's not going to survive the long, retarded prove I'm recommending. In this case, pre-shape it again, or shape once using flour and then shape again following a 30-minute bench rest.

When ready, dust your proving basket with plenty of white flour. Then shape the loaf as you prefer – I like my San Francisco sourdoughs to be round (see pages 62–3) because that's what I've always made, but they can be any shape or size you want. Stick the loaf in its proving basket and then place it inside a plastic bag to keep it hydrated.

Rest for 1 hour at warm room temperature – about 25°C (77°F), if you can. Then, stick the loaf in the fridge, covered with a plastic bag, and leave it for 12–18 hours, or until you can't wait any longer. Don't go longer than 24 hours or so if you want the loaf to maintain any sort of shape. If you are looking for even more tang than this loaf provides, use an older or less well-fed starter, or retard the first prove.

About 30 minutes before you plan to bake, turn your oven on, or even slightly earlier if you're using a baking stone. Preheat it to at least 250°C (480°F)/230°C (450°F) fan/Gas 9. If you're baking in a pot or Dutch oven, you can preheat this, too. I think it gives a slightly better rise and flavour.

Dust a peel or tray with semolina and a little flour. Turn out your loaf and give it a score – I like a simple, single score if it's a batard shape (see pages 64–5), or a square pattern if we're talking about a boule (see pages 62–3). Slide your loaf onto your baking surface and add steam either by spraying the loaf and stone or putting a cast-iron pan filled with water in the bottom of the oven and closing the door. If using a pot, just put the lid on.

Bake for 20 minutes and then vent the oven by opening the door, or remove the lid from your pot. Keep baking for another 20–30 minutes; I wouldn't take the crust too dark. Just enough. Once done, leave to cool for at least 30 minutes before touching.

Danish rye
(rugbrød, or seeded pumpernickel)

Works with leftover starter

For 1 shallow loaf in a 900g (2lb) tin:
350g wholemeal (wholewheat) rye flour, plus extra for dusting
150g rye flakes (cracked rye kernels)
100g rye sourdough starter
350g tepid water
100g sunflower seeds
50g flax or sesame seeds
7g table salt
butter, for greasing
seeds, porridge (rolled) oats or rye flakes, for topping

In a large bowl, weigh your rye flour and your rye flakes. Then add your starter and your tepid water, and mix everything together until roughly combined. An autolyse is extremely important here, as it lets the wholemeal grain properly absorb the water. Leave it a couple of hours at room temperature.

During the autolyse, weigh your sunflower and flax or sesame seeds. Stick them on a tray and place in a non-preheated oven. Set it to 200°C (400°F)/180°C (350°F) fan/Gas 6, and cook the seeds for just 5 minutes or so. They should smell aromatic without being roasted. Leave them to cool. After your autolyse, add the salt to your dough and give it a knead for 3–4 minutes (see pages 47–51) – this isn't always done traditionally, but I find it really helps with the lightness of your final loaf. You'll find the gluten developing and the dough holding its shape far better. At this point, add your cooled seeds and mix until they are evenly combined.

Cover your bowl and leave your dough somewhere at room temperature. I'd prove for 3–4 hours; not too long, as your starter will have got stuck into the fermentation already. I'd do at least one stretch and fold (see page 55),

more for the purposes of redistributing moisture, as water can leach out of this dough and sit on top.

You might not notice much of a rise, but there should be something. Use a dough scraper to turn the dough out onto an unfloured surface and pre-shape (see page 60) into a single lump. Leave it to rest for 20–30 minutes. Meanwhile, grease your loaf tin with plenty of butter.

After your bench rest, lightly flour your surface with rye flour and flip your dough onto it. Shape it very gently into a baton shape (see pages 64–5) – if you press too hard you'll simply tear the structure. Gently transfer it to your tin, seam side down. Place your tin inside a plastic bag and leave it at room temperature for about 2 hours, or until notably bigger again. Alternatively, for epic and earthy flavour, you can retard this loaf in the fridge, covered, to bake the next day.

Despite this being in a tin, I still like to stone bake my loaf, so I preheat my oven to 250°C (480°F)/230°C (450°F) fan/Gas 9 at least 30–40 minutes before I'm expecting it to be ready. If you're not using a stone, 10–15 minutes will do.

Sprinkle with seeds, oats or rye flakes. Usually there's no need to score. Place your tin in the oven and turn the temperature down to 220°C (430°F)/200°C (400°F) fan/Gas 7. Add some steam: I pour water into a cast-iron pan on the floor of the oven. Vent the steam from the oven after 20 minutes, and bake for another 25–30 minutes after that for one large 950g (2lb) loaf tin, or another 10 minutes for half-size 450g (1lb) loaves.

Following this, remove from the oven, bash the loaf out of the tin and place back in the oven for 5–10 minutes, for slightly crustier sides. Cool for at least an hour before slicing.

Brioche

For 2 shallow tins of brioche, or 12 wee 'à tête':
200g white sourdough starter
500g strong white flour
10g table salt
50g caster (superfine) sugar
5 large eggs, at room temperature
150g milk
200g unsalted butter, softened, plus extra for greasing
1 egg, beaten with a pinch of salt, for brushing

Check your sourdough starter about 8–14 hours before you want to bake. It should be very active. If it isn't, take it out of the fridge, give it a feed and see how it does. In any case, let your starter warm up for a couple of hours before using.

In a large bowl, weigh your flour. Add your salt and sugar, and then mix these in using your fingers. Add in your sourdough starter, and then break in your eggs. Warm your milk until it is tepid-warm and mix everything together until you've got a very rough dough. Leave it to sit for 30–40 minutes somewhere warm.

Mix your dough – preferably in an electric mixer. If it's sticky, that's OK. You want it to get to the point where it's silky smooth and stretchy, and is no longer sticking to your hands or the sides of the bowl. Once it's there, you can add the butter, which should be soft. If it isn't, give it a blast in the microwave (it doesn't matter if it's a bit melted). Mix your butter in and keep working until the dough is shiny, smooth and consistent.

Cover your bowl with a plate or damp tea towel and leave it at room temperature for 3–4 hours. This will further develop your gluten and begin

to form some aeration. You could move straight to shaping after this step, but I prefer to let the flavour develop for a little longer. Stick your dough in the fridge, covered, or somewhere cool, and leave it to prove for another 8–12 hours. At some point, grease either two 900g (2lb) loaf tins or 12 small brioche tins with butter.

Following your cold prove, you'll find the dough a rather solid lump, and this is fine. This makes it more tenacious, less extensible and less elastic. Divide into two lumps. Shape into balls just as you would normally pre-shape (see page 60) using your dough scraper. Place these balls in your baking tins – either stacked side by side in 900g (2lb) loaf tins or in your brioche tins. If you've got brioche tins and you like the little ball on top, you'll need to split off little lumps of dough to go on top. As before, shape these just like you'd pre-shape any loaf.

Place the tins in a plastic bag. Leave to prove in a warm place for 2–3 more hours – you want them to grow significantly. If you see little activity, get more heat on it. With the warming up from the fridge, it could take 4–5 hours if your house is cool. About 20 minutes before you think they will be ready, preheat your oven to 250ºC (480ºF)/230ºC (450ºF) fan/Gas 9. Preheat for longer if you're using a baking stone underneath your tins.

Brush the egg wash over the top of your risen brioche. You could sprinkle on sesame seeds if you're feeling fancy, but I don't. Stick your tins in the oven and turn it down to 220ºC (430ºF)/200ºC (400ºF) fan/Gas 7. Bake for about 40 minutes, or until they're not burnt, but getting very dark. Check on them after 30 minutes and turn down the oven by 20ºC/70ºF/two gas marks if you're worried they're colouring too fast. Leave to cool in the tins for at least half an hour, then bash them out to finish cooling on a rack – and they must cool completely before slicing, so don't be tempted to do so sooner.

Demi-baguettes à l'ancienne

For 4 demi-baguettes:
100g white sourdough starter
400g strong white flour, plus extra for dusting
8g table salt
280g tepid-warm water (see method)
semolina, for dusting

The night before you bake, take your starter out of the fridge. If it hasn't been fed recently, feed it by mixing in equal weights of flour and water, to double the size of the starter.

In a large bowl, weigh your flour. Add in your salt and mix these roughly to combine. Mix together some warm and cold water in a jug until it feels just warmer than tepid, about 25°C (77°F), then weigh out 280g and add this along with your sourdough starter to your flour. Mix using a wooden spoon, a dough hook or your hands until you've got a lumpy, messy dough.

Let your dough rest – autolyse – for approximately 30 minutes. You'll want to cover the bowl with a wet tea towel or a plate to stop the dough drying out.

Knead your dough for 5–8 minutes, or until it is starting to become smooth and supple; see the kneading guides on pages 47–51. Baguettes are made with quite a dry dough traditionally, so they have strength by default. You do not need to knead it as much as you do a wet dough – indeed, if you overdevelop the gluten, you'll have tight baguettes that don't rise.

Leave your dough, covered, for 4–5 hours. This will vary depending on temperature. The dough should become very bubbly in this time.

Use a dough scraper to scrape your dough out onto a clean, unfloured surface. Use the scraper to chop the dough into four equal pieces – you can weigh them if you're feeling finicky. To get a real burst of oven spring, baguettes benefit from a pre-shape (see page 60). Rest for 30 minutes following this.

Shape your baguettes. Start by flouring a couche or tea towel, and placing this on a baking tray. Then, following the shaping guide on pages 66–7, create tight, sausage-shaped pieces of dough. After shaping, place your baguette on your couche using a fold in the material to stop neighbouring doughs touching.

Prove for 30 minutes at room temperature, and then move your tray into the fridge. You should cover your baguettes if possible – dusting the tops with a little flour and then laying some cling film (plastic wrap) over the top will be adequate. Prove in the fridge for 8–14 hours, or until you are ready to bake.

Ideally baguettes should be stone baked. If you have baking stones, make sure to preheat your oven at least 40 minutes before you plan to bake. Regardless of what you're using, preheat your oven to 250°C (480°F)/230°C (450°F) fan/Gas 9. If you are using a baguette tray or a baking tray, don't worry too much about it – you'll still have good results. Dust a tray or peel with semolina.

One by one, turn each baguette from your floured couche onto your semolina-covered peel or tray. Each one should now be upside down compared to how it was proved. Score each one down its length, either with one, two or three slashes. Each score should overlap the last by one third, and each one should be almost parallel to the side of the dough – that's how straight. Your blade should be held at an angle, just to break the skin.

Slide your baguettes onto the hot baking stone and add steam – either by pouring water into a cast-iron pan sitting in the bottom of the oven, or by spraying the baguettes and stones with water. Turn down your oven to 230°C (450°F)/210°C (410°F) fan/Gas 8. If you have a fan oven and can turn the fan off, then do so.

Bake for 15 minutes, and then open the oven door to let any excess steam out (remove your cast-iron pan if it still has any water in it). Bake for a further 20–25 minutes, or until the baguettes are a deep chestnut brown. Cool on a rack before enjoying.

Focaccia integrale

For 1 large focaccia:
150g rye or wholemeal (wholewheat) sourdough starter
425g strong white flour
8g table salt
350g tepid-warm water (see method)
100g good-quality extra virgin olive oil, plus extra for oiling
and drizzling
2–3 tsp good-quality sea salt flakes
herbs or toppings as you see fit – I like a handful of olives,
a few tomatoes on the vine, a sliced red onion or a
sprig or two of rosemary

Ideally, take your starter out of the fridge at least 8–14 hours before you want to bake. If it hasn't been fed recently, give it a feed when you take it out. You can use it straight from the fridge, but your first prove will take quite a bit longer.

In a large bowl, weigh your flour. Add the table salt, then mix this in using your fingers. Add in your sourdough starter. Mix some warm and cool water in a jug to 25°C (77°F), then weigh out 350g and pour this into your bowl. Mix everything roughly until you have a very wet dough.

Let the dough rest for about 20–30 minutes – even allowing for a short autolyse of 10 minutes makes a difference. Cover the bowl with a damp tea towel or a plate to stop the dough drying out during this time.

Knead your dough – for this dough (which is very wet), stretching and folding intermittently works very well (see page 55), but I'd still give it a little bit of working before adding the oil. The slap and fold method (see pages 50–51) also works well. Give it 5 minutes of mixing, and as soon as it feels smooth, add your oil. Mix this until completely combined and you've got a very soft, shiny dough.

Wrap your bowl in a couple of large tea towels to keep it warm and stop the dough drying out. Leave in a relatively warm place for about 4 hours. Alternatively, you could retard this prove overnight in a cool place, covering the dough with a plastic bag. I would do a stretch and fold following this, if so, then leave it in a warm place for 1 hour before shaping.

This dough should appear large and slightly terrifying, with loads of big bubbles. If it isn't, leave it a little longer. Once it is, oil a roasting tin and then add a little oil on top of your proven dough. Your hands should be very oily, too. Use your hands or a dough scraper to scrape your dough out of the bowl and into the tin. If it sticks, don't worry – you can lift it off with your scraper and then add more oil.

Flatten your dough slightly, being careful to maintain its delicate air bubbles. Fold your dough in half, and then fold your new, longer dough in half again. I think of this like folding an A4 (US letter) piece of paper twice so that you've got a smaller piece of paper. Add more oil if it's sticking, and gently push your dough out into the corners of a 30 x 40cm (12 x 16in) roasting tin.

Stick your tin inside a plastic bag and leave to prove for 2–3 more hours at room temperature. Alternatively, you can retard this prove overnight or for up to 24 hours until your bread is ready to bake. You want it to grow further by about half.

Preheat your oven to 250ºC (480ºF)/230ºC (450ºF) fan/Gas 9 at least 30–40 minutes before you expect to bake your bread. If you have a stone, place it in the oven to heat up. Just before it's ready to bake, remove the focaccia from the plastic bag and poke indentations using oiled fingers in the dough, giving the focaccia its characteristic holes. Top with some flaked sea salt, at least, and any olives, vegetables or herbs you like. Drench the whole thing with generous drizzles of oil.

Place in the oven and add steam using your chosen method – for example, adding some water into a cast-iron pan that's sitting in the bottom of the oven. Turn the oven down to 220°C (430°F)/200°C (400°F) fan/Gas 7. Bake for 20 minutes, and then vent the oven by opening the door and allowing the steam to escape. Bake for another 15–20 minutes, or until a good golden brown.

Leave to cool for at least 15 minutes. Then add more oil on top. Slice and serve hot if you like, but it does also keep extremely well. Just add more oil when you serve it.

Neapolitan-style pizza

For 4 pizzas:
100g white sourdough starter
400g strong white flour (preferably Italian '00' pizza flour),
plus extra for dusting
7g table salt
260g tepid water
plenty of semolina, for dusting (flour will do, though)

For the topping:
3 garlic cloves
1 tbsp good olive oil
400g tomato passata (sauce)
salt and freshly ground black pepper
2 x 125g balls of mozzarella
cured meat or salami (optional)
a handful of fresh basil leaves (optional)

It's best to make your dough at least 24 hours before you plan to make pizza. The dough keeps for 3–4 days, at least, and I know those who always have a supply of sourdough pizza dough in the fridge, just in case. Make sure your starter is nice and healthy, and that the majority of it consists of white flour.

Make the dough. In a large bowl, weigh out your flour and add the table salt. Mix these together to combine, then add the tepid water and starter. Use a wooden spoon to combine everything into a wet and sticky dough. Cover the bowl, then leave it for at least 1 hour at room temperature.

While you could mix this dough vigorously, we don't want to overdevelop the gluten. It should remain soft and sticky. I'd do a couple of stretches

and folds (see page 55), and watch it rise over about 6–8 hours at room temperature. It should be very bubbly and sticky. At this point, cover with a plastic bag, put it in the fridge and leave it. It can be left for up to 3–4 days, albeit becoming slightly tangier each day. It's best used between 24 and 48 hours.

Before it's time to bake, get organised. Make your pizza sauce – peel and finely chop your garlic and place this in a pan with the oil. Gently infuse over the lowest heat for 5 minutes (don't burn it). Add your passata, stir and turn up the heat to simmer. Add salt and pepper to taste. This can be prepared in advance and chilled, if you like. Chop your mozzarella into slices and place this in some kitchen paper (paper towels), or wrap in a cloth, to dry.

While some people like to pre-shape their pizza dough to make a very round disc, I'm a bit more rustic. Dust the work surface with plenty of semolina and a little flour, or just flour if you don't have any semolina. Turn your dough out on top, and then add more semolina and flour again. Divide your dough using a scraper into four equal lumps, and coat each of these with semolina, too. It's not possible to use too much. Once your doughs are divided and your toppings are prepared, you can preheat your grill (broiler) as hot as it goes with the door as close to closed as possible, and then get a cast-iron pan or surface onto your hob (stovetop) to heat as hot as you dare.

Work quickly. Dust some semolina on a tray or peel. Take a piece of dough and stretch it flat. Don't use a rolling pin. Throwing the dough in the air and spinning it really does help. You want the centre of the dough almost translucent, and you should leave a 1-cm (½-in) thick rim around the edge to give a good puff and stop the sauce leaking. Place this on your peel. Give the peel a good shake to make sure the dough isn't sticking. Add more semolina if it does. Spread some sauce on top, no more than 3–4 tablespoons, and then a quarter of your mozzarella and some slices of cured meat or salami, if using. Add a few fresh basil leaves, if you like. Give it another shake to make sure it isn't stuck.

Gently slide this onto your smoking hot pan. Use thick, thick oven gloves to move this under your grill, and shut the door (or close it as much as possible if your grill turns off when you shut it). Cook for 2 minutes, then check it. You want the edges of the crust to be just about blackening, and the cheese melted and bubbling but not browning. Keep going if it isn't. Lift up the edge to check underneath. If it's still soggy on the bottom but done on top, put it back on the hob for a minute or two. For the next pizza (if the first wasn't quite cooked underneath) you can leave it on the hob for up to a minute before placing under the grill.

Enjoy hot, as fresh as humanly possible. It takes the sacrifice of one person to make the family's pizza, but it's so worth it. Between each pizza, get your surface back on the hob to heat up to frightening levels again before you slide your next pizza on top. The dream is to have two surfaces, for back-to-back pizzas, for ever.

Pretzels

For a dozen large pretzels:
400g strong white flour, plus extra for dusting
220g tepid water (see method)
150g white sourdough starter
7g table salt
sea salt flakes, for sprinkling

For the bath:
1 litre cold water
20g lye (caustic soda), or 50g bicarbonate of soda (baking soda)

In a large bowl, weigh your flour. Mix together some warm and cold water in a jug until it feels just warmer than tepid, about 25°C (77°F), then weigh out 220g and add this along with your sourdough starter to your flour. This is a very dry dough. Mix using a wooden spoon, a dough hook or your hands until you've got one solid lump.

Let your dough rest for approximately 30 minutes – this autolyse, without salt, really helps when managing such tenacity. Cover the bowl with a damp tea towel or a plate to stop the dough drying out.

Add your table salt, then knead your dough for 10–15 minutes, or until it is properly shiny and smooth. The best way to do this is in a stand mixer, to be honest, but otherwise the English knead (see page 49) will work well. Like with bagels, the pretzel is aided by a good lot of kneading.

Leave your dough, covered, for 3 hours or so at room temperature. Your proving time will vary depending on temperature. Don't worry about any stretching and folding – it doesn't need it. The dough should be plenty strong enough. Lightly flour a work surface. Use a dough scraper to move your dough out onto it and then use floured hands to gently roll it out into a big doughy sausage. Use your scraper to chop this into 12 equal pieces – you can weigh them if you want to be conscientious. Prepare two trays by coating them with a tea towel or cloth and flouring it, or by lining with non-stick greaseproof baking paper.

You should start like you would with a baguette (see pages 66–7). Sprinkle a little flour onto the surface and place your first piece of dough on top. Fold each piece like an A4 (US) letter going into a windowed envelope: first the side towards you, and then the side away from you. Tighten it further into a very tight sausage, then use the open palms of your hands to roll this dough backwards and forwards. Keep a chunky bit in the middle about 2.5cm (1in) thick, but then taper it each side into thin spindles. The total length should be about 40cm (16in), ideally.

Shape the dough into an upside-down 'U', with the swollen bit in the middle at the curve of the 'U'. Twist the two ends around each other two or three times, leaving at least a few centimetres of each strand free at the end. Then invert your 'knot', and press each free end onto the edge of the main body of your bagel. Place on your cloth- or paper-covered trays and repeat.

Leave your pretzels to prove for an hour or so – no more. This gives you time to clear some space in the freezer. Freezing is an optional step that helps the pretzels hold their shape much better in their caustic bath. Ideally, put your trays of pretzels in the freezer for 30 minutes before dunking.

Before you start your bath, preheat your oven to 220ºC (430ºF)/200ºC (400ºF) fan/Gas 7. Pretzels are fine just baked on baking trays, as we're not after a supremely crisp base. About 20 minutes of preheating will be plenty.

Prepare your bath. Don rubber gloves (NOT nitrile or latex) and goggles, and fill a bowl (stainless steel, glass or hard plastic) with the cold water. Add your lye and stir gently until it has completely dissolved – **always add lye (caustic soda) to water, never add water to caustic soda**, otherwise

the exothermic reaction as it dissolves will cause dangerous spluttering. If you're using bicarb (baking soda), weigh it out and stick it on a baking tray, then bake during your 30 minutes of pretzel freezing in your preheating oven. Stir to dissolve this in your water.

Using a gloved hand or a stainless-steel slotted spoon, dip each frozen pretzel into your lye. Hold it here for 5 seconds, and then remove it, letting any excess drip away. If using baked bicarb, leave it in the bath for roughly 20–30 seconds before draining. Place each nearly-dry pretzel on a new baking tray, preferably lined with some non-stick greaseproof baking paper. (You can take your gloves off now.)

Use a lame or razor to score the thick part of all your pretzels and then sprinkle with plenty of sea salt. Place your trays in the oven to bake for about 15–20 minutes. They should be a deep and shiny golden brown, almost like they're dipped in plastic, with a magnificent pale 'ear'. Cool for at least 10 minutes before eating.

NB: Caustic solution can be poured down the plug hole to dispose of it – it'll even take care of any blockages in your drain. Just don't splash. Any drips may discolour your natural stone or wooden work surfaces.

Crispbread

Works with leftover starter

For 6–8 large crispbreads:
150g wholemeal (wholewheat) rye flour, plus extra for rolling
*   and stretching*
150g unbleached strong white flour
175g tepid water
150g white sourdough starter
5g table salt
2–3 tbsp crushed wheatgerm, or nuts or seeds, for topping

In a bowl, weigh your two flours. Add in your water, and mix this together until you've got a stiff dough. Cover the bowl and leave this for about 8–12 hours. At the same time, take your sourdough starter out of the fridge and feed it.

After this time, add the sourdough starter to your dough, as well as the salt. Mix everything together until you've got something that's consistent. You don't need to work it really hard. You don't even have to knead it, but using something like the English knead (see page 49) might help in bringing the ingredients together. Once the dough is uniform, stop. Stick it back in the bowl and cover.

Prove for 6–8 hours at a cool room temperature. Don't chill it in the fridge so that it is cold – this will make stretching a little harder, and it won't ferment quite so well. Your crackers would be leathery rather than crisp.

Preheat your oven to as hot as it goes – usually 250ºC (480ºF)/230ºC (450ºF) fan/Gas 9. You want to do this at least 40 minutes before you aim to bake if you've got a baking stone. If not, 10 minutes will do.

Generously flour a work surface using rye flour, and tip your dough out onto it. Move it around to coat with flour and add more if necessary. Do add some more flour on top. Chop your dough into six or eight roughly equal chunks – don't be sticking wee bits of chopped floury dough together to make it more even; whatever size the chunks come out at is fine.

Use floured hands to stretch each chunk of dough until it is as thin as you can make it. We're talking really thin – if possible, almost translucent. Use flour to stop them sticking. Then use a rolling pin to get them even thinner. If you're struggling, you can place the tough dough in the fridge for a few minutes as you start the next one. Once rolled, you can bake them in whatever shape they come out at, or you can cut them into large circles using a plate and a knife, and cut small holes in the centres to facilitate breaking into portions.

Slide a peel or baking sheet under your crispbread and use a fork to prick all over: this stops it forming one massive air pocket. Gently brush the top of the crispbread with some water, and then sprinkle with some crushed wheatgerm or press your seeds into the top. Slide your crispbreads into your oven or bake on a tray and bake for 6–8 minutes, or until they turn a dark golden brown. They might take a bit longer if the thinness isn't quite there. Repeat until you've got none left. Note that they won't be 100% crisp until they've cooled – this will take approximately 10 minutes.

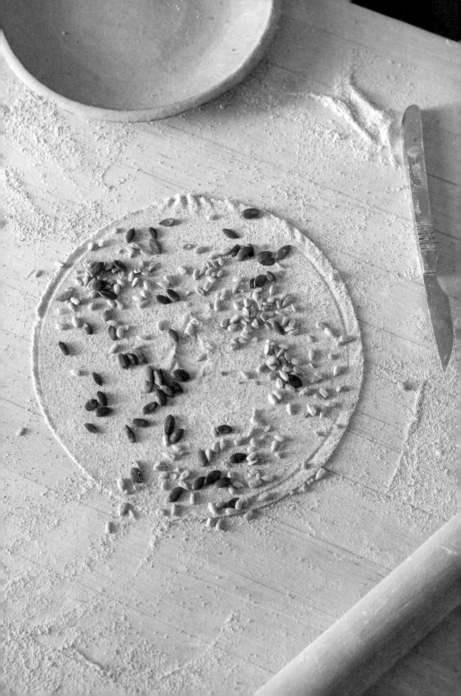

Index & suppliers

Index

Suppliers

The wonderful bowls, plates and fermentation jars you see are handcrafted by **Natalie Smith**, whom you can find at @throwing_pots on Insta, and you can email her for orders on throwingpots@posteo.uk.

BakeryBits.co.uk is where I get most of my baking stuff. It has everything, including wonderful unbleached **Gilchester's** flour and the tricky but flavourful **Lammas Fayre** biodiverse selection of ancient grains.

For the majority of the recipes in this book we used **Marriage's** strong white flour, supplied by **Fitzbillies** bakery in Cambridge. Head there for the quintessential Chelsea Bun. Most recently, I've been ordering big sacks straight from **Shipton Mill**: their Number 4 flour is absolutely delicious and can cope with a decent long prove.

The best electric mixer I've used and owned comes from Denmark, and it is the **Varimixer** Teddy (varimixer.com). It strengthens dough similar to stretches and folds. The specific dough scrapers used in the shoot are **Campbell's Dough Knives**, and you can find him on Insta @campbell2664 or rackmaster.co.uk. They're excellent.